A BIBLIOGRAPHY OF THE LITERATURE DEALING WITH THE CENTRAL INDIA AGENCY

A BIBLIOGRAPHY OF THE LITERATURE DEALING WITH THE CENTRAL INDIA AGENCY

C. ECKFORD LUARD

GYAN

Published by

Gyan Publishing House
5, Ansari Road
Daryaganj, New Delhi-110002
Phone: 011-47034999, 9811692060
E-mail: books@gyanbooks.com

Distribution Network
gyanbooks.com
India, USA, Canada, UK, Australia

ISBN: 978-93-7447-878-3 (PB)

First Published, 1908

2nd Impression 2026

Printed at: Gyan Press, Delhi.

A BIBLIOGRAPHY OF THE LITERATURE DEALING WITH THE CENTRAL INDIA AGENCY

Author: C. ECKFORD LUARD

A

BIBLIOGRAPHY OF THE LITERATURE

DEALING WITH

THE CENTRAL INDIA AGENCY,

TO WHICH IS ADDED

A SERIES OF CHRONOLOGICAL TABLES,

BY

CAPTAIN C. ECKFORD LUARD, M.A. (Oxon), I.A.,
Superintendent of Gazetteer in Central India.

Published by Order of His Majesty's Secretary of State for India in Council.

LONDON:
PRINTED BY EYRE AND SPOTTISWOODE,
PRINTERS TO THE KING'S MOST EXCELLENT MAJESTY.

1908.

CONTENTS.

PREFACE.

This Bibliography for Central India professes to be no more than a local handbook. Save for a few recent works which have lately come to my notice, it is merely a classified list of such books and papers as I met with in my reading for the Gazetteer work.

That the Bibliography, which is merely the result of a single individual's research, is absolutely complete I do not for a moment pretend, but it will, I trust, serve as a basis for a fuller work, and will at least give a clue to all the more important publications and papers dealing with the history, archæology, &c., of Central India.

In the Historical and Archæological Section all the books and papers deal more or less with Central India, but in other sections they are necessarily of a general charactor.

If this Bibliography proves of some use to officials and others in Central India who desire a closer acquaintance with the sources of information available, but have not the leisure to ransack libraries, it will have attained its object.

I would add for the convenience of those in the Agency, that almost all the books and all the journals can be obtained from the Library of the Bombay Branch of the Royal Asiatic Society, as any member, by paying small extra subscription, can have publications sent to him up country. Most of the works are, moreover, purchaseable second hand, those *scarce* or *rare* are marked **[S]** and **[R]**.

My thanks are due to the Secretary of State for India in Council for kindly sanctioning the issue of this book.

C. E. L.

London, September 1908.

3642. I. 1284. 250.—11/1908.

ABBREVIATIONS USED IN CHRONOLOGICAL TABLES AND BIBLIOGRAPHY.

A. C.	Aufrecht's Catalogus Catalogorum.
A. S. N. I.	Archæological Survey of Northern India (2 vols.).
A. S. W. I.	Archæological Survey Reports of Western India (5 vols.).
As. Qu. Rev.	Asiatic Quarterly Review.
BEAL *Records*	Buddhist Records of the Western World, by S. Beal.
B. F.	Briggs' Translation of Ferishta's History (4 vols.).
B. G.	E. C. Bayley's History of Gujarat.
B. Mem.	Babar's Memoirs, by W. Erskine, London, 1829.
B. M. C.	British Museum Catalogues of Coins.
B. R.	Dr. Bhandarkar's Reports on the search for Sanskrit MSS.
Cal. Rev.	Calcutta Review.
C. A. S. R.	Archæological Survey Reports, by Sir A. Cunningham.
C. I. I.	Corpus Inscriptionum Indicarum.
EARLY HIST.	The Early History of India, by V. A. Smith, 1904.
E. I. or EP. IND.	The Epigraphia Indica.
E. M. H.	Sir H. M. Elliott's History of India as told by its own Muhammadan historians (8 vols.).
G. D.	Grant Duff's History of the Mahrattas (2 vols., 1878).
I.A. or IND. ANT.	The Indian Antiquary.
J. A.	Journal Asiatique (Paris).
J. A. B. or J. B. A.	Journal of the Asiatic Society of Bengal.
Pr. J. A. B.	*Proceedings* of the Asiatic Society of Bengal.
J. A. O. S.	Journal of the American Oriental Society.
J. B. R. A. S.	Journal of the Bombay Asiatic Society.
J. R. A. S.	Journal of the Royal Asiatic Society, London.
Num. Chr.	Numismatic Chronicle, London.
P. R.	Reports on the search for Sanskrit MSS., by Dr. Peterson (4 vols.).
Rajasthan	The Rajasthan by Colonel J. Tod. Calcutta Reprint, in 2 vols., 1893.
R. T.	The Tabakāt-i-Nāsiri, translated by Major Raverty.
T. P. K.	E. Thomas's Pathan Kings of Delhi.
V. O. J. or W. Z. K. M.	The Vienna Oriental Journal or Wiener Zeitschrift für die kunde des Morgenlandes.
W. H. T.	The Hindu Theatre, by H. H. Wilson.
W. V. P.	Wilson, W. H. *Vishnu Purána*, edited by F. E. Hall.
Z. D. M. G.	Zeitschrift der Deutschen morgenländischen Gesellschaft.

Note.—Where no town of publication is given *London* is implied, except in the case of publications by the Government or Local Governments in India.

BIBLIOGRAPHY.

SECTION I.

GENERAL.

(1.)—Bibliographies and Catalogues.

(i.) Orientalische Bibliographie. Edited by Dr. Lucian Scherman. (Berlin.)

(ii.) Luzac, publisher and seller of Oriental works. His book catalogues are most useful.

(iii.) Bernard Quaritch. His lists of books are invaluable. No. 205 refers especially to Oriental works.

(iv.) Nicholas Trübner, publisher. His lists of books are most valuable.

(v.) Cambray, publisher, Hastings Street, Calcutta. His lists are full of Oriental works.

Many second-hand booksellers' lists are also useful in this respect, such as George & Co., Bristol, Edwards, High Street, Marylebone.

(vi.) Catalogue of the Library of the Bombay Branch of the Royal Asiatic Society. (Rs. 12.)

(2.)—Journals of Asiatic Societies, &c.

[N.B.—*These journals constantly contain papers of importance regarding Central India, especially the first four.*]

(i.) Journal of the Royal Asiatic Society of London.

(ii.) Journal of the Asiatic Society of Bengal. (Calcutta.)

(iii.) Journal of the Bombay Branch of the Royal Asiatic Society. (Bombay.)

(iv.) The Indian Antiquary. (Bombay Education Society's Press, Bombay.)

(v.) Journal Asiatique. (Paris.)

(vi.) Journal of the American Oriental Society. (New York.)

(vii.) Zeitschrift der Deutschen Morgenländischen Gesellschaft. (Berlin.)

(viii.) Wiener Zeitschrift fur die kunde des Morgenlandes. Vienna Oriental Journal. (Vienna.)

(ix.) Numismatic Chronicle.

(x.) Giornale della Societa asiatica orientale. (Rome.)

(xi.) Reports of the Oriental Congresses (various).

(xii.) Journal of the Royal Society of Arts.

(xiii.) The Imperial and Asiatic Quarterly Review.

(xiv.) Journal of the Bombay Natural History Society. (Bombay.)

(xv.) The Epigraphia Indica (for inscriptions, &c.).

Other journals and magazines occasionally have papers of interest on Central Indian subjects.

(3.)—Government Publications.

[N.B.—*This List includes those of a general or current description only, more particular issues appear under Archæology, &c.*]

(i.) Administration Reports for the Central India Agency from 1865 to 1903.

(ii.) Administration Reports for individual States from 1904 onwards.

(iii.) Archæological Survey Reports :—

- (*a*) Of Sir A. Cunningham, Vols. II., VII., IX., X., XIII., XVIII., XX., XXI.; Index by V. A. Smith. (1887.)
- (*b*) Of Government of India Archæological Department from 1903.
- (*c*) Of Provincial Circles, Progress Reports, &c.
- (*d*) Archæological Reports for Western India, 5 volumes.

(iv.) Census Reports for Central India, 1881, 1891, 1901.

(v.) Census Report for Gwalior State, 1901.

(vi.) Enactments of British India in force in Stations, &c., in Native States. By J. M. Macpherson. (Calcutta, 1893.)

(vii.) Gazetteers :—

- (*a*) Imperial. (New edition of 1908.)
- (*b*) Provincial issue of Imperial Gazetteer, for Central India.
- (*c*) State series of Gazetteers for Central India, including the States of—
  - Vols. I.–IV. Gwalior, Indore, Bhopāl, Rewah.
  - Vol. V. Dhār, Barwāni, Jhābua, and Ali-Rājpur; Dewās, Jaora, Ratlām, Sītamau, and Sailāna; Rājgarh and Narsinghgarh.
  - Vol. VI. Orchha, Datia, Samthar, Charkhāri, Chhatarpur, Bijāwar, and Panna.
- (*d*) Provincial Gazetteers :—
  Of those Provinces which border on Central India, viz., Bombay, Central Provinces, United Provinces, and Rājputāna.

(viii.) Hemp Drug Commission, 1893–94, Report of.

(ix.) Nimār, Report on the Province of. (Rurki, 1856.)

(x.) Nimār, Settlement of. (Rurki, 1848.)

(xi.) Opium, Report on the Consumption of. Parl. Papers, 1893.

(xii.) Search for Sanskrit MSS. (The Bombay Circle Reports are of more local interest for Central India than those of Calcutta, but all are useful.)

(xiii.) Thornton's (E.) Gazetteer of the Territories of the East India Company and of the Native States. Four volumes. 1854. (Invaluable.)

(xiv.) Treaties, Sanads, and Engagements, Calcutta. Vol. IV. Central India, Mālwā; Vol. VI. Bundelkhand. Compiled by Sir C. Aitchison. (Under revision).

(4.)—Encyclopedias, Dictionaries, &c.

(i.) AUFRECHT, TH. Catalogus Catalogorum. An alphabetical register of Sanskrit works and authors. (Leipzig, 1891.)

(ii.) BALFOUR, E. Cyclopedia of India. 5 Vols. (Madras, 1872.)

(iii.) BANESS, J. F. Index Geographicus Indicus. 1881.

(iv.) BEALE, T. W. Oriental Biographical Dictionary. Revised by H. G. Keene. (1894).

(v.) BUCKLAND, C. E. Dictionary of Indian Biography. (1906.)

(vi.) CROOKE, W. Rural and Agricultural Glossary. (Calcutta, 1888.)

(vii.) Constable's Hand Atlas of India. (1893).

(viii.) Dictionary of National Biography. Edited by Leslie Stephen and Sidney Lee. 63 Vols. (1903.)

(ix.) DOWSON, J. Classical Dictionary of Hindu Mythology. (1891.)

(x.) Grundriss der Indo-Arischen Philologie und Altertumskunde. Edited by G. Bühler. (Partly German and partly English). (Trübner.) (Strassburg, 1896.)

(xi.) JEPPEN, J., S.J. An Historical Atlas of India. (Longmans & Co.) 1908.

(xii.) NANDA LAL DE. Geographical Dictionary of Ancient and Mediæval India. (Calcutta).

(xiii.) Old Map in Massie's "Continental India" (interesting). 1840.

(xiv.) WILSON, H. H. Glossary of Judicial and Revenue Terms. (1855.)

(xv.) YULE AND BURNELL. A glossary of Anglo-Indian terms. (Hobson Jobson.) (New edition.) 1903.

(5.)—Vernacular Texts, Edited or Translated.

[*The Summaries of Edited Texts are useful, especially for Paramara History.*]

BALLALA :—

(i.) Bhoja-prabandha. Edited by K. Pandurang. Narayan-sagar Press. (Bombay, 1896.)

BANA :—
(ii.) Sri-Harsha-Charita. Translated by Cowell and Thomas. (1897.)
(iii.) Kādambari. Translated by C. M. Ridding. (1896.)

BILHANA :—
(iv). Vikramānkādeva Charita, Edited by G. Bühler with Summary. (Bombay, 1875); review, I. A., ii., 317.

CHAND BARDAI :—
(v.) Prithvirāj Raso. (Medical Hall Press. Benares, 1904.)

DHANIKA :—
(vi.) Dasharupa. Edited by F. E. Hall, with Introduction. (Calcutta, 1865.)
(vii.) Hammiramahākāvya. Edited by N. J. Kirtane, with Summary. (Bombay, 1879.)

GHORPURE, J. R. :—
(viii.) Mahārāstra Itihās. (History of the Marathas).

KALIDASA :—
(ix.) The Mālavikagnimitra. Translated by C. H. Tawney. Thacker. (Calcutta, 1891.)

KHARE, V. S. :—
(x.) Aitihāsik lekh sangrāha (Maratha historical documents).

KRISHNAMISRA :—
(xi.) Prabodhachandrodaya. Translated by J. Taylor. (1812.)

MUIR, J. :—
(xii.) Original Sanskrit Texts. 5 Vols. (Trübner.) (1861–84.)

PARIMALA :—
(xiii.) Navasāhansānka Charita. Translated by Bühler and Zachariae. I. A., xxxvi., 162.

RAJASEKHARA :—
(xiv.) Kapura-manjari. Translated by Konow and Lanman. Harvard Oriental Series. No. IV. (1901.)

RAJWADE, V. K. :—
(xv.) Peshwyānchi Shakāwali. (Diary of the Peshwas).

SOMESHVARA :—
(xvi.) Kirtikaumudi (Text and Summary). Edited by Kāthvate. Bombay Sanskrit Series. (1883.)
(xvii.) Surathotsava. Edited by Devadatta and Pandurang Parab. (Bombay, 1702.)

VAD, G. C. :—
(xviii.) Shāhu Maharāj Yānchi Rojānshi. (Diary of Rāja Shāhu).

VAKPATI :—
(xix.) Gaudavaho. Edited by S. P. Pandit. (Bombay, 1887).

VALLABHADEVA :—
(xx.) Subhashitāvali. Edited by J. Peterson, with Summary. (Bombay, 1886); review, I.A., xv., 240.

SECTION II.

GEOGRAPHY AND HISTORY.

(1.)—Early Period, 700 B.C. to 970 A.D.

[*N.B.—As it is impossible to separate Early History and Archæology, a reference to the Index is essential in searching for a paper in this Section.*]

BOOKS.

BEAL, S.:—
(i.) Buddhist records of the Western World. 2 Vols. (Trübner.) (1884.)
(ii.) Travels of Fah-Hian. (1869.)

BHANDARKAR, R. G.:—
(iii.) Early History of the Deccan. (Bombay, 1884.)

CUNNINGHAM, SIR A.:—
(iv.) The Ancient Geography of India, Buddhist period. (1871.)

DUFF, C. M.:—
(v.) The Chronology of India. (1899.)

DUTT, R. C.:—
(vi.) A history of civilization in Ancient India. 2 Vols. (Trübner.) (1894.)

DUTT, M. N.:—
(vii.) The Mahābhārata, a translation. (Elysium Press, Calcutta.)

ELPHINSTONE, M.:—
(viii.) History of India. (New edition.) (1905.)

GROWSE, F. S.:—
(ix.) Mathura. (Third edition.) (1883.)

JULIEN, S.:—
(x.) Hioun Thsang. Memoires sur les Contrées Occidentales. (Paris, 1857.)
(xi.) Histoire de la vie de Hioun Thsang. (Paris, 1853.)

LASSEN, CHR.:—
(xii.) Indische Alterthumskunde. 4 Vols. (Bonn and Leipzig, 1867.)

LEGGE, J.:—
(xiii.) The Travels of Fa-Hien. (Oxford, 1886.)

LUARD, C. E. and LELE, K. K.:—
(xiv.) The Paramāras of Mālwā in Appendix to Dhār State Gazetteer (1908), and reprinted separately. (Bombay, 1908.)

MANNING, MRS. :—
(xv.) Ancient and Mediaeval India. 2 Vols. (1869.)

MARSHMAN, J. C. :—
(xvi.) The History of India (abridged). (Blackwood.) (1880.)

MCCRINDLE, J. W. :—
(xvii.) (Series on Ancient India) :—
(*a.*) Ancient India as described by Megasthenes and Arrian. (Bombay, 1877.)
(*b.*) Ancient India as described by Ktesias the Knidian. (Bombay, 1882.)
(*c.*) Ancient India as described by Ptolemy. (Bombay, 1885.)
(*d.*) The Navigation of the Erythrean Sea. (1879.)
(*e.*) Strabo, Herodotus, &c.
(*f.*) The Invasion of India by Alexander. (1896.)

PALLÉ, F. :—
(xviii.) Cartografia antica dell' India. Pamphlet. (Oriental Congress.) (1868.)

RAGOZIN, Z. :—
(xix.) Vedic India. (Stories of the Nations.) (Unwin.) (1902.)

RAWLINSON, G. :—
(xx.) The History of Herodotus. 4 Vols. (1858.)

RHYS-DAVIDS, T. W. :—
(xxi.) Buddhist India. (Stories of the Nations.) (Fisher-Unwin.) (1903.)

SACHAU, C. E. :—
(xxii.) Albiruni's India. (Trübner.) 2 Vols. (1879.)

ST. MARTIN :—
(xxiii.) Memoire Analytique sur la Carte de Asie Centrale et de l'Inde. (Paris, 1858.)

SMITH, V. A. :—
(xxiv.) The Early History of India. (1st edition, 1904; 2nd edition, 1908.)
(xxv.) Asoka. (Rulers of India.) (Oxford, 1901.)

STEIN, M. A. :—
(xxvi.) Kalhana's Rājatarangini, or Chronicles of the Kings of Kashmir. 2 Vols. Text and translation. (1901.)

VINCENT, W. :—
(xxvii.) The Commerce and Navigation of the Ancients in the Indian Ocean. 3 Vols. (1809.)

PAPERS.

BHAGVANLAL INDRAJI :—
(xxviii.) The Western Kshatrapas. J. R. A. S., xxii., 639.

BHANDARKAR, D. R. :—
(xxix.) Gurjaras. J. B. R. A. S., xxi., 413.

BHANDARKAR, R. G. :—
(xxx.) A Peep into the early History of India. J. B. R. A. S., xx., 356.

BÜHLER, G. :—
(xxxi.) Hwen Thsiang's Account of Harshavardhana. I. A., vii., 196.

BURGESS, J. :—
(xxxii.) Geography of India, with an extract from a paper by the late H. H. Wilson. I. A., xx., 418.

FLEET, J. F. :—
(xxxiii.) On Hoernle's Article on Indian History. J. R. A. S., 1904, 164.

GROWSE, F. S. :—
(xxxiv.) The Poems of Chand-Bardai. J. A. B., xxxvii. (i.), 119; xxxviii. (i.), 1.

HALL, FITZ-E. :—
(xxxv.) Vestiges of the Royal House of Kanykubja. J. A. B., xxxi., 1.

HEMACHANDRA, Dvaiasharaya of, a Synopsis of contents :—
(xxxvi.) I. A., iv., 71, 110, 232, 265.

HOERNLE, A. F. :—
(xxxvii.) Gaharwars and Rāthors. I. A., xiv., 98.
(xxxviii.) Some Problems of Ancient Indian History. J. R. A. S., 1903, 545; 1905, 1.
(xxxix.) The Gurjara Empire. J. R. A. S., 1904, 639.

KENNEDY, J. :—
(xl.) The Early Commerce of Babylon with India. J. R. A. S., 1898, 241.

PARGITER, F. E. :—
(xli.) Ancient Chedi, &c. J. A. B., lxiv. (i.), 249.
(xlii.) The Nations of India at the Battle between the Pandavas and Kauravas. J. R. A. S., 1908, 311.

REHATSEK, H. :—
(xliii.) An Old Map of the World. I. A., i., 369.

RHYS DAVIDS, T. W. :—
(xliv.) Early Commerce between India and Babylon. J. R. A. S., 1899, 432.
(xlv.) Asoka and the Buddhist Relics. J. R. A. S., 1901, 397.

SCANLAN, H. :—
(xlvi.) A Sketch of Umri. I. A., iii., 231.

SLEEMAN, Col. W. H. :—
(xlvii.) The Gond Rajas of Mandala. J. A. B., vi., 621.

SMITH, V. A. :—
(xlviii.) Samudra Gupta. J. R. A. S., 1897, 19.
(xlix.) The Conquests of Samudra Gupta. J. R. A. S., 1897, 859.
(l.) The Kushān Period. J. R. A. S., 1903, 1.
(li.) The History of Bundelkhand. J. A. B., l., 1.

WATSON, J. :—
(lii.) Historical Sketch of Pāwagarh. I. A., vi., 1,

(2.)—Muhammadan Period, 970–1707 A.D.

BOOKS.

BALL, V.:—
(i.) Tavernier's Travels. 2 Vols. (1889.)

BAYLEY, E. C.:—
(ii.) The History of Gujarat. (1886.)

BALWANT RAO BHAYA:—
(iii.) History of the Fortress of Gwalior. (Bombay, 1892.)

BLOCHMANN and JARRETT:—
(iv.) The Ain-i-Akbari of Abul Fazal. (Calcutta, 1873–94.) [S.]

BRIGGS, Col. J.:—
(v.) The History of the Rise of the Muhammadan power in India. 4 Vols. (1829.) (Reprint is being issued by Cambray, Calcutta.) [S.]

CATROU, F.:—
(vi.) Histoire generale de l'Empire du Mogol. (Paris, 1715.)

CONSTABLE, A.:—
(vii.) Bernier's Travels. (Translated.) (1891.)

COURTEILLE, A. P.:—
(viii.) Memoires de Bābar. 2 Vols. (Paris, 1871.)

DOUGLAS, J.:—
(ix.) Bombay and Western India. 2 Vols. (1892.)

DOW, A.:—
(x.) The History of Hindostan. 3 Vols. (1792.)

ELLIOT, H. M.:—
(xi.) The History of India, as told by its own Historians. 8 Vols. (1867–77.)

ERSKINE, W.:—
(xii.) Babar's Memoirs. (Translated from the Turki.) (1829.) [R.]
(xiii.) The History of India under the two first sovereigns of the house of Timur. 2 Vols. (1854.)

FOSTER, W.:—
(xiv.) The Embassy of Sir Thomas Roe. (Hakluyt Society, Series 2, Nos. 1, 2.) 2 Vols. (1899.)

FRANCKLIN, W.:—
(xv.) The Reign of Shah Aulum. (1798.)

FRYER, Dr. J.:—
(xvi.) A new Account of East India. (1698.)

HAKLUYT, R.:—
(xvii.) Collection of Early Voyages. 5 Vols. (1809.)

HUSSAIN KHAN:—
(xviii.) Seir-ul-Mutaquherin. 4 Vols. Cambray. (Calcutta.)

IRVINE, W.:—
(xix.) The Army of the Moghuls. (1903.)
(xx.) The Storia di Mogor of N. Manucci. (Translated—Indian Text Series.) 4 Vols. (1907.)

KEENE, H. G. :—
(xxi.) The Moghul Empire from the Death of Aurungzeb. (1866.)
(xxi.) The Fall of the Moghul Empire. (Allen, 1887.)
(xxiii.) The Turks in India. (1879.)

LANE-POOLE, S. :—
(xxiv.) Aurungzib. (Rulers of India.) (Oxford, 1893.)
(xxv.) The Moghul Emperors of Hindostan and their Coins (1892.)
(xxvi.) Bābar (Rulers of India Series). (Oxford, 1899.)
(xxvii.) Mediæval India. ("Stories of the Nations.") (Fisher Unwin.) (1903.)

LEE, S. :—
(xxviii.) The Travels of Ibn-Batuta. (1829.)

MALLESON, G. B. :—
(xxix.) Akbar. (Rulers of India.) (Oxford, 1891.)

MANDELSLO, J. A. :—
(xxx.) Voyages celebres, &c. (Paris, 1727.) [R.]

MANDU :—
(xxxi.) Māndu, the ancient capital of Malwa. By a Subaltern. (Bombay, 1844.)
(xxxii.) Māndu, the History of. (Bombay, 1875.) (Anonymous.)

NOER, F. A., Count :—
(xxxiii.) The Emperor Akbar. Translated and in part revised by Annette S. Beveridge. 2 Vols. (Calcutta, 1890.)

POGSON, W. R. :—
(xxxiv.) A history of the Bundelas. (Calcutta, 1828.)

PRICE, Maj. D. :—
(xxxv.) Memoirs of the Emperor Jahangueir. (1829.)

RAVERTY, Maj. :—
(xxxvi.) Tabakāt-Nāsiri. (Translation.) (1881.)

RENAUD, H. :—
(xxxvii.) Fragments arabes et Perses. (Paris, 1845.)

RYLEY, J. H. :—
(xxxviii.) Ralph Fitch, England's pioneer to India and Burmah. (Unwin.) (1900.)

SACHAU, E. :—
(xxxix.) Albiruni's India (Translated). 2 Vols. (Trübner.) (1879.) [S.]

SARKAR, J. :—
(xl.) The India of Aurungzeb. (Calcutta, 1901.)

SCOTT, J. :—
(xli.) Ferishta's history of the Deckan. 2 Vols. (Shrewsbury, 1794.)

SONNERAT, J. :—
(xlii.) Voyages aux Indes orientales. 3 Vols. (Paris, 1782.)

TERRY, E. :—
(xliii.) Voyage to East India. (1655.) (Reprinted, 1777.)

THEVENOT, M. DE. :—
(xliv.) Voyages contenant la relation de l'Indostan. (Paris, 1684.)

THOMAS, E. :—
(xlv.) The Revenue Resources of the Moghul Empire. (1871.)

TIEFFENTHALER, J. :—
(xlvi.) Description Historique et Geographique de l'Inde Redigé en Francais par M. Jean Bernouilli. (Paris. 1786.)

VALLE, DELLA :—
(xlvii.) Travels of P. Della Valle, (translated) by G. Havers. (1665.) Edited by E. Grey. 2 Vols. (1892.)

WRIGHT, F. N. :—
(xlviii.) The Chandel Thakurs. I. A., ii., 33.

PAPERS.

BEVERIDGE, H. :—
(xlix.) On General Maclagan's paper about the Jesuit Mission to Akbar. Pr: J. A. B., 1903, 123; *ib.*, lxxiii. (i.), 49.
(l.) Donna Juliana. J. R. A. S., 1903, 244.
(li.) A visit to Abul Fazl's grave. Cal. Rev. 110, p. 67.

BÜHLER, G. :—
(lii.) A Jaina account of the end of the Vaghelas of Gujarat. I. A., xxvi., 194.
(liii.) Prithvirāja. Pr: J. A. B., 1893, 94.

DUTT, R. C. :—
(liv.) The Economic Condition of India under Maratha Rule. East and West. i., 18.

HAIG, W. :—
(lv.) Some Historical Indian Famines. As. Q. Rev. 1901, 9.
(lvi.) Some Notes on the Bāhmani Dynasty. Pr: J. A. B., 1904, 76.

HUNTER, W. W. :—
(lvii.) The Ruin of Aurungzeb. Nineteenth Century. May 1887.

IRVINE, W. :—
(lviii.) Note on the Official Reckoning of the Reigns of the late Mughal Emperors. Pr: J. A. B., 1893, 161.
(lix.) The Later Mughals. J. A. B., lxiii. (i.), 112; lxv. (i.), 136; lxvii. (i.), 141; lxxii. (i), 33; lxxiii. (i.), 287.
(lx.) The Regnal Years of Shah Alam Bahadur Shah, &c. Pr: J. A. B., 1904, 50.

KEENE, H. G. :—
(lxi.) The Revenues of the Moghul Empire. J. R. A. S., (N. S)., xix, 495.
(lxii.) Mughals and Turks. Cal. Rev., cv., 180.

KING, J. S. :—
(lxiii.) History of the Bāhmani dynasty. I. A., xxviii., 119, ff.; xxix., 4.

KING, L. W. :—
(lxiv.) History and Coinage of Malwa. Num. Chr., 1904. 62 ff.

MACLAGAN, GEN. :—
(lxv.) The Jesuit mission to the Emperor Akbar. J. A. B., lxv. (i.), 38. (*See ibid*, lxxii., 49 note.)

PATHAK, K. B.:—
(lxvi.) A passage referring to the Guptas in the Jain Harivansa, I. A., xv., 141.

REHATSEK, J.:—
(lxvii.) The reign of Shah Ahmad Durrani. I. A., xvi., 298.

SILBERRARD, C. A.:—
(lxviii.) A contribution to the history of Western Bundelkhand. J. A. B., lxxi. (i.), 99.

YULE, H.:—
(lxix.) The geography of Ibn-Batuta's travels. I. A., iii., 114.

(3.)—Maratha and Modern Period. 1707 A.D. to present day.

BOOKS.

ABERIGH-MACKAY, G. R.:—
(i.) The Chiefs of Central India Vol. I. Indore. (Calcutta, 1879.)
(ii.) Twenty-one days in India. (Calcutta.)

ARCHER, MAJ.:—
(iii.) Tours in Upper India. (1833.) 2 Vols.

ASIATIC ANNUAL REGISTER:—
(iv.) Various papers:—
Vols. III. and VI., on Europeans in Native State service.
Vol. IV., on Gohad.
Vols. V. and VI., on Sindhia's and Holkar's Army, and on Ujjain.
Vol XI., on capture of Ajaigarh.

BEGAM OF BHOPAL:—
(v.) Pilgrimage to Mecca of Nawāb Sikandar Begam. (1870.)

BEVAN, MAJ. H.:—
(vi.) Thirty years in India. 2 Vols. (1839.)

BLACKER, V.:—
(vii.) Memoir of the operations of the British Army during the wars of 1817, 1818, and 1819. 2 Vols. and maps. (1821.)

BOULGER, D. C.:—
(viii.) Lord William Bentinck (Rulers of India). (Oxford, 1892.)

BROUGHTON, T. D.:—
(ix.) Letters written in a Mahratta camp (1809). (Constable, 1893.)

BURNE, O. T.:—
(x.) Clyde and Strathnairn, and the suppression of the great revolt. (Oxford, 1891.)

CALCUTTA REVIEW:—
(xi.) Vol. I., Female Infanticide (372); Gwalior (535); Vol. XXVI., Lucan (561); Vol. XXXVI., Bāndhogarh.

CALENDAR:—
(xii.) The East India Military Calendar, 1823. (Biographies of officers, Popham, Camac, &c.)

CHESNEY, SIR G.:—
(xiii.) Indian Polity. (Longmans.) (1894.)

COLEBROOKE, T. E.:—
(xiv.) Life of Mountstuart Elphinstone. 2 Vols. (1884.)

COMPTON, H.:—
(xv.) A particular account of the European military adventurers of Hindusthan from 1784 to 1803. (Unwin.) (1892.)

COOPLAND, R. M.:—
(xvi.) A lady's escape from Gwalior during the Mutiny. (1859.)

DALY, H.:—
(xvii.) Memoirs of Sir Henry Daly. (1905.)

DAVIDSON, LT.-COL. C. J. C.:—
(xviii.) Diaries of travel in Upper India. 2 Vols. (1843.)

DICKINSON, J:—
(xix.) Dhar not restored, &c. (1854.)
(xx.) Sequel to Dhār not restored. (1865.)
(xxi.) Last counsels of an unknown counsellor. (1877.)
(xxii.) Mr. Dickinson, and Dhār. (1864.)

DUBERLY, MRS.:—
(xxiii.) Campaigning experiences in Rajpootana and Central India. (1859.)

DUFF, J. G.:—
(xxiv.) A history of the Mahrattas. 3 Vols. (1826.)

DURAND, H. M.:—
(xxv.) Life of Sir H. M. Durand. 2 Vols. (1883.)

FITZ-CLARENCE, LT.-COL.:—
(xxvi.) Journal of a route across India. (1819.)

FORBES, J.:—
(xxvii.) Oriental memoirs. (1st edition, 1813.) 2nd edition. 2 Vols. (1834.)

FORBES, A. K.:—
(xxviii.) Rās Māla. 2 Vols. (1856.)

FORSYTH, J.:—
(xxix.) The Highlands of Central India. (Chapman.) (1889.)

FORREST, G. W.:—
(xxx.) Selections from the letters and despatches preserved in the Foreign Department of the Government of India. (1772–85. Goddard's march.)
(xxxi.) Selections from the State papers preserved in the Bombay Secretariat. Maratha Series, Vol. I. (Contains Malet's Diary of his journey through Mālwā in 1784.)

FRANCKLIN, W.:—
(xxxii.) Military memoirs of George Thomas. (Calcutta, 1803.)

FRASER, J. B.:—
(xxxiii.) Military memoirs of Lt.-Col. J. Skinner. 2 Vols. (1851.)

GERARD, SIR M.:—
(xxxiv.) Leaves from the diary of a soldier and sportsman. (1903.)

GLEIG, REV. G. R.:—
(xxxv.) Life of Arthur, Duke of Wellington. 4 Vols. (1858.)
(xxxvi.) Memoirs of the life of the Right Honourable Warren Hastings. 3 Vols. (1841.)

GODDARD, LT.-COL. J.:—
(xxxvii.) Journal of the March of the Bombay Army across the Mahratta country. (1778) [R].

GOODWYN, LT.-COL. H.:—
(xxxviii.) Report on the Agra-Bombay road. (Agra, 1851.)

GRIFFIN, SIR LEPEL:—
(xxxix.) The native Princes of India. (1889.)

GRIFFITH, M.:—
(xl.) India's princes. (Allen.) (1894.)

GURWOOD, LT.-COL.:—
(xli.) Despatches of the Duke of Wellington, 1799–1818. 12 Vols. (1835.)

GWALIOR:—
(xlii.) Gwalior and Lashkar. (Account reprinted from Gwalior Gazetteer.) (Calcutta, 1908.)

HASTINGS, MARQUESS:—
(xliii.) Private Journals of. 2 Vols. (1858.)

HOCKLEY, W. B.:—
(xliv.) Pandurang Hari. 2 Vols. 2nd edition. (1873.)

HODGES, W.:—
(xlv.) Travels in India (1780–83.). (1793.)

HOLMES R.:—
(xlvi.) A history of the Indian Mutiny. (5th edition.) (Macmillan.) (1898.)

HOPE, J.:—
(xlvii.) The House of Scindea. (1863.)

HOUGH, W.:—
(xlviii.) Political and Military Events (1756–9). (1853).
(xlix.) Brief History of the Bhopal Principality. (Calcutta, 1845.)

HUNGERFORD, T.:—
(l.) Report of occurrences at Mhow during the Mutiny. (Privately printed.) (1857.) [R.]

HUNTER, W. W.:—
(li.) The Earl of Mayo. (Rulers of India.) (Oxford, 1891.)

HUTTON, W. H.:—
(lii.) The Marquess of Wellesley. (Rulers of India.) (Oxford, 1893.)

HUTTON, J.:—
(liii.) Account of the Thugs. (1857.)

ILBERT, C. :—
(liv.) The Government of India. (Oxford, 1898.)

JACQUEMONT, V. :—
(lv.) Correspondence pendant un voyage dans l'Inde. 2 Vols. (Paris, 1832.)
(lvi.) Voyages dans l'Inde (1828–32). 6 Vols. (Paris, 1846.)

JONES, MAJ. H. :—
(lvii.) The Campaign of Lord Lake against the Marathas. (1881.)

KAYE, J. W. :—
(lviii.) The Lives of Indian Officers. 3 Vols. (1889.)
(lix.) The Life of Sir John Malcolm. 2 Vols. (1856.)

KAYE J. and MALLESON, G. B. :—
(lx.) History of the Indian Mutiny. 6 Vols. (Longman.) (1878–88.) Also Index by F. Pincott in separate volume.

KEENE, H. G. :—
(lxi.) Mādhava Rao Sindhia. (Rulers of India.) (Oxford, 1892.)

LEE-WARNER, SIR W. :—
(lxii.) The Protected Princes of India. (Macmillan.) (1984.)

LETHBRIDGE, R. :—
(lxiii.) The Golden Book of India. (Macmillan.) (1893.)

LOWE, T. :—
(lxiv.) Central India during the Rebellion of 1857. (1860.)

LLOYD, SIR W. :—
(lxv.) Narrative of a Journey from Caunpore to the Boorendo Pass. 2 Vols. (1846.)

LYALL, SIR A. :—
(lxvi.) The Rise and Expansion of the British Power in India. (Murray.) (1893.)

MACDONALD, A. :—
(lxvii.) The Life of Nana Furnavese. (Bombay, 1851.)

MACPHERSON, MAJOR S. C. :—
(lxviii.) Memorials of Service in India (of), by W. Macpherson. (1865.)

MAHRATTA AND PINDAREE CAMPAIGN :—
(lxix.) Summary of the Mahratta and Pindaree Campaigns. (1820.)

MALCOLM, J. :—
(lxx.) Memoirs of Central India. 2 Vols. (Calcutta, 1881.)
(lxxi.) The Political History of India from 1784–1823, 2 Vols. (1826.)
(lxxii.) Report on the Province of Mālwā. (Calcutta, 1822.) (This is the basis of the book on Central India.)

MALLESON, G. B. :—
(lxxiii.) The History of the French in India. (Allen.) (1893.)
(lxxiv.) Essays and Lectures. (1866–76.)
(lxxv.) The Native States of India. (1873.)
(lxxvi.) Final Struggles of the French in India. (1884.)
(lxxvii.) The Marquess Wellesley. (1889.)

MARTIN, MONTGOMERY :—
(lxxviii.) The History of the Possessions of the East India Company. 2 Vols. (1837.)

MASSEY, J. W. :—
(lxxix.) Continental India. 2 Vols. (1840.)

MILL, J. :—
(lxxx.) The History of British India. (Edited by H. H. Wilson.) 10 Vols. (1858.)

MINTURN, R. B. :—
(lxxxi.) New York to Delhi. (New York, 1858.)

MUNDY, G. C. :—
(lxxxii.) Pen and Pencil Sketches in India. 2 Vols. (1832.)

MUTINY IN INDIA :—
(lxxxiii.) Narrative of events regarding the. 3 Vols. (Official.)
(lxxxiv.) Selections of State Papers. (Calcutta, 1893.)

NOER, F. A., COUNT :—
(lxxxv.) The Emperor, Akbar. Translations in part revised by Annette S. Beveridge. 2 Vols. (Thacker.) (Calcutta, 1890.)

ORME, R. :—
(lxxxvi.) Historical Fragments. (1805.)

OWEN, S. J. :—
(lxxxvii.) A Selection from the Despatches of the Marquis Wellesley during his Government of India. (Oxford 1877.)

PARKES, F. :—
(lxxxviii.) The Wanderings of a Pilgrim in search of the Picturesque. 2 Vols. (1850.)

PARASNIS, D. B. :—
(lxxxix.) Diaries of the Satara Raja's and Peshwas. (In Marathi, with Summaries.) (Several issues. Sahasrakar Press, Poona.)

POSTANS, MRS :—
(xc.) Western India. 2 Vols. (1839.)

PRICHARD, J. T. :—
(xci.) The Mutinies in Rajputana (1857). (1860.)

PRINSEP, H. T. :
(xcii.) Memoires of the Pathaun Soldier of Fortune . . . . Ameer Khan . . . . from the Persian of Busawan Lal. (Calcutta, 1832.) [S.]
(xciii.) The history of the military and political transactions during the adminstration of the Marquess Hastings 2 Vols. (1825.)

RAINES, SIR J. :—
(xciv.) The campaign in Central India, 1857. (1900.)

RENNELL, J. :—
(xcv.) Memoirs of a Map of Hindusthan. (1783.)

ROSS OF BLADENSBURG :—
(xcvi.) The Marquis of Hastings. (Rulers of India.) (Oxford, 1893.)

ROUSSELET, L. :—
(xcvii.) L'Inde des Rajas. (Paris, 1875.)

SCOTT, P. G. :—
(xcviii.) Personal Narrative of the Escape from Nowgong (privately printed). (Edinburgh, 1857.) [**R**]

SETON-KARR, W. S. :—
(xcix.) The Marquess of Cornwallis. (Rulers of India.) (Oxford, 1890.)

SHERER, COL. G. M. :—
(c.) Sketches of India, written by an Officer for fireside travellers. (1824.)

SYLVESTER, SURG. J. S. :—
(ci.) Recollections of the Campaign in Malwa and Central India under Sir Hugh Rose. (Bombay, 1860.)

SLEEMAN, W. H. :—
(cii.) The Rambles and Recollections of an Indian Official. (Constable.) (1893.)

SMITH, L. F. :—
(ciii.) A Sketch of the Rise, Progress, and Termination of the Regular Corps. (Calcutta, 1805.)

STRACHEY, SIR J. :—
(civ.) India. (1894.)

SONNERAT, M. :—
(cv.) Voyages aux Indes Orientals. 3 Vols. (Paris, 1782.)

SURENDRA, N. R. :—
(cvi.) Gwalior. (Calcutta, 1888.)

SUTHERLAND, J. :—
(cvii.) Sketches of the Relations subsisting between the British Government and the different Native States. (1833). (Reprint, 1837.)

THEVENOT, J. :—
(cviii.) Voyages en Europe, Asie, et Afrique. 5 Vols. (Amsterdam, 1727.)

THORN, W. :—
(cix.) The War in India (1803–06). (1818.)

THORNTON, T. H. :—
(cx.) Sir Richard Meade and the Feudatory States of Central and Southern India. (1898.)
(cxi.) The History of the British Empire in India. 6 Vols. (1841.)

TOD, J. :—
(cxii.) The Annals and Antiquities of Rajasthan. Reprint. (Calcutta, 2 Vols., 1899). [Original edition of 1832, rare.]
(cxiii.) Travels in Western India. (1839.)

TONE, W. H. :—
(cxiv.) Institutions of the Mahratta people. (Bombay, 1798.) [**R**]

TROTTER, L. S. :—
(cxv.) Warren Hastings. (Rulers of India.) (Oxford, 1890.)

TUPPER, SIR C. L. :—
(cxvi.) Our Indian Protectorate. (1893.)

TWINING, T. :—
(cxvii.) Travels in India a Hundred Years Ago (1795). (1893.)

VALENTIA, VISCOUNT :—
(cxviii.) Voyages and Travels to India, &c. 3 Vols. (1809.)

WELLESLEY, MARQUIS :—
(cxix.) The History of the Maratha War, 1803. (1804.)

WELLINGTON :—
(cxx.) Military History of the Duke of, in India. (1852.)

PAPERS.

BARR, SIR D. :—
(cxxi.) Progress in Native States, &c. Journal Royal Society of Arts. 20th March 1908.

BURNE, OWEN :—
(cxxii.) Lord Strathnairn. As. Qu. Rev., 1886, 52.

CLAUDE MARTIN, E. W., MAJ.-GEN. :—
(cxxiii.) Calc. Rev., Vol. 93, 98.

FENWICK, W. :—
(cxxiv.) The Nerbudda from Dhari Falls to Haranphal. J. A. B., xvii., 210.

FERRAND, G. :—
(cxxv.) Les Bourbons de l'Inde. Revue de Paris, 1905, v., 189.

GRIFFIN, LEPEL :—
(cxxvi.) The Native Princes of India. As. Qu. Rev., viii., 209; ix., 17.
(cxxvii.) The rendition of Gwalior Fort. As. Qu. Rev., 1886, 4.

KEATINGE, LIEUT :—
(cxxviii.) Report of a passage made on the Nerbudda. J. A. B., xvi., 1104.

KINCAID, COL. W. :—
(cxxix.) The Indian Bourbons. As. Qu. Rev., 1887. 164.

IRVINE, W. :—
(cxxx.) Etymology of the word Pindhari. I. A., xxix., 140.

LEE-WARNER, SIR W. :—
(cxxxi.) The Native States of India. International. Quart. vi., 178.

MAHARAJPUR :—
(cxxxii.) Maharajpur, battle at. Cal. Rev., Vol. 8, 535.

MALLESON, G. B. :—
(cxxxiii.) Famous women of India. As. Qu. Rev., Jan. 1887, 57.

MONSON, COL. :—
(cxxxiv.) Defeat of, and assistance given by Lucan. Cal. Rev., xxvi., 567.

MUTINY, in newspapers :—

(cxxxv.) (*Only detailed notices are given here*) :—

(*a*) "Delhi Gazette" Newspaper. Mutiny accounts :—
(i) June issue gives account of Nīmach.
(ii) Rewah and Panna. In November issue. (1857.)

(*b*) "Mofussilite" Newspaper of Agra. Mutiny accounts :—
(i) Gwalior. Issue of 19th August 1857.
(ii) Agar. Issue of 5th September.
(iii) Nowgong. Issue of 17th October.
(iv) Mandasor. Issue of 29th January 1858.
(v) Sipri. Issue of 19th August; part of Gwalior account.
(vi) Mehidpur. Issues of 1st and 29th December.

(*c*) "The Times" Newspaper. Letters of personal experiences in the Mutiny, sent to :—

Of 1857 :—
(i) Agar. 1st August.
(ii) Gwalior. Issues of 25th and 26th August, — September, 5th October, 18th November.
(iii) Indore. 25th August (Native letter); 2nd, 5th, 7th, 28th September.
(iv) Mhow. 18th August; 8th September.
(v) Nimach, 8th September; 1st, 18th November.
(vi) Nowgong. 11th September.
(vii) Sipri. 11th September.

Of 1858 :—
(i) Proclamation of Firoz Shah. 7th May.
(ii) Tantia Topi at Rajgarh. 28th October.
(iii) Interview with Tantia Topi. 8th December.

Of 1859 :—
(i) Native's interview with Tantia. 19th May.
(ii) Sipri letters of 18th April, 20th May.

OLDENBUCK, A. :—
(cxxxvi.) Madhoji Sindia. Academy. 21st February 1888.

OWEN, S. J. :—
(cxxxvii.) Benoit de Boigne. Eng. Hist. Rev. (January 1888), 63.

PAPERS :—
(cxxxviii.) Respecting the Maratha and Pindaree Wars. Published by E. I. C. (1824.)

PANIPAT :—
(cxxxix.) The battle of. (1761). Asiatic Researches, iii, 91.

PARASNIS, D. B. :—
(cxl.) Maratha Historical Literature. J.B.R.A.S., xxii., 168.

PETER, F. L. :—
(cxli.) The progress and prospects of the Native States of Central India. As. Qu. Rev., 1888, 156.

SECTION III.

RELIGION, ETHNOLOGY, &c.

BOOKS AND PAPERS.

AYNSLEY, M. A.:—
(i.) A paper on Stone Implements, Celts, &c. I. A., xv., 117.

BADEN-POWELL, B. H.:—
(ii.) Notes on the Origin of the "lunar" and "solar" Aryan Tribes. J. R. A. S., 1899, 295, 519.

BARNES, E.:—
(iii.) The Bhils of Western India. Jour. Royal Society of Arts, Feb. 1907.

BARTH, A.:—
(iv.) The Religions of India. (Trans.) (Trübner.) (1889.)

BELNOS, S. C.:—
(v.) The Sandhya (a series of coloured plates). (Allahabad, 1881.)

BENDALL, C.:—
(vi.) Ancient Indian Sects mentioned by Buddhist Writers (Parivrā-jaka). J. R. A. S., 1901, 122.

BHANDARKAR, R. G.:—
(vii.) The History of Child Marriage. Z. D. M. G., xlvii., 143.

BÜHLER, G.:—
(viii.) The Authenticity of Jaina Tradition. W. Z. K. M., i., 165; ii., 141.
(ix.) Further Proof of the Authenticity of the Jaina Traditions. W. Z. K. M., iv. 313.
(x.) The Digambara Jains. I. A., vii., 28.
(xi.) Uber das Leben des Jaina Monches Hemachandra. (Wien, 1889.)
(xii.) On the Indian Sect. of Jainas. (Luzac.) (1903.)

BURGESS, J.:—
(xiii.) The Buddhist Mudras. I. A., xxvi., 24.
(xiv.) Note on Jaina Mythology. I. A., xxx., 27.
(xv.) Digambara Jain Iconography. I. A., xxxii., 459.
(xvi.) The Navagraha. I. A., xxxiii., 61.

CARNEGY, J.—
(xvii.) The Bhars of Audh and Benares. J. A. B., xlv., 297.

COWELL, E. B.:—
(xviii.) The Swayamvara of the Ancient Hindus, &c. J. A. B., xxviii., 31.

CROOKE, W. :—
(xix.) Popular Religion and Folk-lore of Northern India. 2 Vols. (Constable.) (1896.)
(xx.) The Hill Tribes of the Central Indian Hills. Jou. Anthro. Inst. of Great Brit. and Ireland., xxviii., 220.

CUMBERLEDGE, N. R. :—
(xxi.) Some Account of the Bunjarrah Class. (Bombay, 1882.)

DALTON, COLONEL E. F. :—
(xxii.) Descriptive Ethnology of Bengal. 2 Vols. (Calcutta, 1872.) [S].

DESHMUKH, G. M. :—
(xxiii.) On the Habits of the Jain Ascetics. J. Anthro. Soc. Bom., i., 2.

DRACOTT, A. :—
(xxiv.) Folk-lore from Central India, &c. (Allahabad Pioneer Press, 1897.)

DRESSNER, H. :—
(xxv.) Folk-lore from Central India. (Pioneer Press, Allahabad.)

DRIVER, W. H. :—
(xxvi.) The Korkus. J. A. B., lxi. (i), 128.

DUBOIS, J. A. :—
(xxvii.) Hindu Manners, Customs, and Ceremonies. (Translated by H. K. Beauchamp.) 3rd edition. (Oxford, 1906.)

DYER, H. :—
(xxviii.) Pandita Ramabai, the story of her life. (Revell.) (New York, 1900.)

ELLIOT, H. M. :—
(xxix.) Memoirs of the History, Folklore, &c., of the North Western Provinces. J. Beames. 2 Vols. (1869.)

FALLON, S. W. :—
(xxx.) Dictionary of Hindusthani Proverbs. (Benares, 1884.)

FAUSBOLL, V. :—
(xxxi.) Indian Mythology. (Luzac). (1903.)

FAWCETT, M. S. :—
(xxxii.) Infant Marriage in India. Contemp. Rev. Nov. 1890. 712.

FEMALE INFANTICIDE :—
(xxxiii.) Parliamentary Papers on, 1824, 1828, 1843. (*See also* Cal. Rev. i., 372.)

FERGUSSON, J. :—
(xxxiv.) Tree and Serpent Worship, 1868.

GOSH, P. C. :—
(xxxv.) On Snake Symbols. J. A. B., xlviii. (i), 30.

GRIFFIN, SIR LEPELL :—
(xxxvi.) The Bhils and their Country. A. Q., Rev. vii., 438.

GRIMTHORPE, J
(xxxvii.) Notes on Criminal Tribes, 1882.

GROWSE, F. S.:—
(xxxviii.) Mathura. (N. W. P. Government Press, 1883.)

GRÜNWEDEL, A.:—
(xxxix.) On the Aghoris (in German) Zeitschrift fur Ethnol, xx., 307.
(xl.) Buddhist Art in India. (1901.)

GUPTE, B. A.:—
(xli.) Female Tattoo Designs in India. I. A., xxxi., 293.
(xlii.) Female Tattooing at Vindhyachal. I. A., xxxiii., 117.

HARDY, R. S.:—
(xliii.) A Manual of Buddhism. (1880.) (2nd edition).

HAUG, H.:—
(xliv.) Essays on the Sacred Literature, Worship, and Religion of the Parsis. (1884.)

HISLOP, Rev. S.:—
(xlv.) The Aboriginal Tribes of the Central Provinces. (Nagpur, 1866).

HOERNLE, A. F. R.:—
(xlvi.) Pattâvali of the Upakesa Gachha (Oswâls). I. A., xix., 233.
(xlvii.) Three further Pattâvalis of the Digambaras. I. A., xxi., 57.

HOPKINS, E. W.:—
(xlviii.) The Religions of India. (Ginn & Co.) (Boston, 1902.)
(xlix.) India, Old and New. (Scribner.) (New York, 1901.)
(l.) Land Tenure in Ancient India. Political Science, Quarterly. 1898.

HUGHES, T. P.:—
(li.) A Dictionary of Islam. (1885.)

JACKSON, A. V. W.:—
(lii.) Kalidâsa at Ujjain, &c. J. A. O. S., xxii., 321; xxiii., 307.

JACOB, H.:—
(liii.) Die Jaina legende. Z. D. M. G., xlii., 493.

JACOB, G. A.:—
(liv.) A Manual of Hindu Pantheism. (Trübner.) (1889.)

KERN, H.:—
(lv.) Histoire du bouddhisme dans l'Inde (Paris, 1903.)

KITTS, E. J.:—
(lvi.) Castes and tribes of India. (Bombay, 1885.)

KLATT, J.:—
(lvii.) Extracts from the Jain historical records. I. A., xi., 245.
(lviii.) The Mânbhavas. I. A., xi., 22.

LUARD, C. E.:—
(lix.) Tattooing in Central India. I. A., xxxiii., 219, 237, 280, 301.
(lx.) A collection of brass from Central India. I. A. 1908.

LUDERS, H.
(lxi.) Indische Höhlen als Vergnügen Sorte. Z.D.M.G., lviii., 867. (*See* I. A., xxxiv, 197.)

LYALL, SIR A. :—
(lxii.) Asiatic Studies. 2 Vols. (Murray.) (1899.)

MACKENZIE, J. :—
(lxiii.) Tree and serpent worship. I. A., iv., 5.

MACRITCHIE :—
(lxiv.) The gypsies of India. (1886.)

MAINE, SIR H. S. :—
(lxv.) Village communities in east and west. (1876.)

MANWARING, A. :—
(lxvi.) Marathi proverbs. (Oxford, 1899.)

MOOR, E. :—
(lxvii.) The Hindoo Pantheon. (Original edition, 1811) [R]. (Reprint, Madras, 1864.)
(lxviii.) Hindoo infanticide. (1811.)

MOOZAMDAR. :—
(lxix.) The faith and progress of the Brahmo-Samaj. (Calcutta, 1882.)

MUIR, W. :—
(lxx.) The life of Mahomet. (1877.)

MULLER, F. MAX :—
(lxxi.) India: What can it teach us? (New edition.) (Longmans.) (1892.)

MURRAY-AYNSLEY, J. :—
(lxxii.) Asiatic symbolism. (Celts and sacred stones). I. A., xv., 117.

NESFIELD, J. :—
(lxxiii.) The caste system of the North-Western Provinces. (Allahabad, 1885.)

OMAN, J. C. :—
(lxxiv.) The Mystics, Ascetics, and Saints of India. (Unwin.) (1905.)
(lxv.) Brahmans, Muslims, and Theists of India. (1907.)

OPPERT, G. :—
(lxxvi.) On the Weapons, Army, &c., of the Ancient Hindus. (Madras, 1880.)

R. B. :—
(lxxvii.) Hindu castes among Marathas. Calcutta Review, cxv., 21.

REHATSEK, H. :—
(lxxviii.) Translation of Lassen's account of the Jainas. I. A., ii., 193, 258.

RISLEY, H. H. :—
(lxxix.) Note on some Indian Tatu Marks. "Man." 1902. 97.
(lxxx.) Infant Marriage. Blackwood Mag., cxlviii., 785.
(lxxxi.) The Tribes and Castes of Bengal. Anthropometric data. 4 Vols. Calc., Government Press.

ROST, R. :—
(lxxxii.) Thugs (article on). Encycl. Britt., Vol. xxiii.

RUSSELL, N. :—
(lxxxiii.) Village work in India. (Oliphant.) (New York, 1902.)

SAINT HILAIRE :—
(lxxxiv.) Le Bouddha et sa religion. (Paris, 1862.)

SENART, E. :—
(lxxxv.) Les castes dans l'Inde. Rev. des Deux Mondes. cxxi., 506 ; cxxii., 94.

SHERRING, REV., M.A. :—
(lxxxvi.) Hindu tribes and castes. 3 Vols. (Calcutta, 1881.)

SEWELL, J. :—
(lxxxvii.) The Indian boomerang. J. R. A. S., 1898, 379.

SLEEMAN, COL. W. H. :—
(lxxxviii.) Report on the Thug gangs of India. (Calcutta, 1840.)
(lxxxix.) Illustrations of the methods and practice of Thugs. (1851.)

SMYTH, H. W. :—
(xc.) Weber's sacred literature of the Jains. I. A., xvii, 279, 339 ; xviii, 181.

TEMPLE, R. C. :—
(xci.) Glimpses into a Bhil's life. I. A., xxi., 123.

THEOBALD, J. :—
(xcii.) Stone celts, &c. J. A. B., xxxi., 323.

TILAK, B. G. :—
(xciii.) The arctic home in the Vedas. (Bombay, 1903.)

VAL D'EREMAO, J. P.
(xciv.) An Indian Rajah at home ; a sketch from real life. As. Qu. Rev., II. Ser. iv., 7, 181.

VASUDEV BIRJE :—
(xcv.) Who are the Marathas? (Bombay Nirnaya Sagar Press, 1899.)

WARD W. :—
(xcvi.) An account of the writings, religion, and manners of the Hindoos. (Serampur. 4 Vols. 1811.)

WATSON, J. :—
(xcvii.) The derivation of "Mehwāsi." I. A., vi., 79.

WEST, E. W. :—
(xcviii.) Are the Marathas Kshatrias. I. A., iii., 108.
(xcix.) Divine Mothers and local goddesses of India. I. A., x., 245.

WIGHT, J. K. :—
(c.) The Cosmogenies of India and China. J. A. O. S., 1890, lxiv..

WILLIAMS, MONIER :—
(ci.) Hinduism. (1877.)

WILSON, H. H. :—

(cii.) The Vishnu Purana. Edited by F. E. Hall. 6 Vols. (1864.)

(ciii.) A sketch of the religious sects of the Hindus. (Calcutta, 1846.)

WILSON, J. :—

(civ.) Indian Castes. (1877.)

SECTION IV.

ARCHÆOLOGY, NUMISMATICS, EPIGRAPHY, &c.

BOOKS.

BURGESS, J.:—
(i.) Iconography of the Digambara Jains. (Bombay, 1904.)

CATALOGUE OF INDIAN COINS:—
(ii.) In the Calcutta Museum.
(iii.) In the Lahore Museum.

CHOISY, A.:—
(iv.) Histoire de l'Architecture. 2 Vols. (Paris, 1903.)

COLEBROOKE, T. E.:—
(v.) Life and Essays of H. T. Colbrooke. 3 Vols. (1873.)

CUNNINGHAM, SIR A.:—
(vi.) Archæological Survey Reports:—
Vol. II. Gwalior, Chanderi, Khajrāho, Dhamnār, &c.
Vol. VII. Malwa and Bundelkhand.
Vol. IX. Baghelkhand.
Vol. X. Malwa and Bundelkhand.
Vol. XIII. Baghelkhand.
Vol. XVIII. Baghelkhand.
Vol. XIX. Baghelkhand.
Vol. XX. Gwalior.
Vol. XXI. Malwa and Bundelkhand.
[General Index by V. A. Smith in separate vol.]
(vii.) The Stupa of Bharhut. (1879.)
(viii.) The Bhilsa Topes. (1854.) [S.]
(ix.) Corpus Inscriptionum Indicarum: Vol. I.—Asoka's inscriptions.
(x.) Coins of ancient India from the earliest times to seventh century A.D. (Quaritch.) (1891.)
(xi.) The coins of the Indo-Scythians. (Luzac, 1882.)
(xii.) Coins of Mediæval India. (Quaritch.) (1894.)
(xiii.) The book of Indian eras. (Calcutta, 1883.)

FERGUSSON, J.:—
(xiv.) On the Study of Indian Architecture. (1867.)
(xv.) Illustrations of the Rock-cut Temples. 2 Vols. (1845.)
(xvi.) Picturesque illustrations of Ancient Architecture in Hindostan. (1848.) [S.]
(xvii.) Tree and Serpent Worship. (1868.)
(xviii.) Indian and Eastern Architecture. (New edition, 1908.)

FERGUSSON and BURGESS:—
(xix.) The Cave Temples of India. (1880.) [S.]

FLEET, J. F. :—
(xx.) The Gupta inscriptions forming Vol. III. of the *Corpus Inscriptionum Indicarum.*

FOUCHER, A. :—
(xxi.) Etude sur l'iconographie Bouddhique de l'Inde. (Paris, 1905.)
(xxii.) L'Art Greco-Bouddhique de Gandhara. Vol. I. (Paris, 1905.) (Under issue.)

GRIFFITH, J. :—
(xxiii.) The paintings in the Buddhist caves of Ajanta. 2 Vols. 1896.

GUIAND, J. :—
(xxiv.) The Ruins of Mandoo. (Reprint of text from Harris's book.) (Dhār, 1892.)

HARRIS, CAPTAIN C. :—
(xxv.) The Ruins of Mandoo. (Coloured illustrations.) (1860.)

IMPEY, DR. E. :—
(xxvi.) Description of the Caves of Khoolve (Kholvi) in Malwa. (Agra, 1853.)

LANE-POOLE, S. :—
(xxvii.) Indian Coins in the British Museum. 3 Vols. (1884 to 1892.)

MAISEY, E. C. :—
(xxviii.) Sanchi and its Remains. (1892.)

MODAK :—
(xxix.) Chronological Tables (giving dates day by day for Hindu, Muslim, Shuhur eras, and A.D.) from 1728 to 1889. (*In Hindi.*) (Vidyavdas Press, Poona, 1889.)

PRINSEP, J. :—
(xxx.) Essays and Useful Tables. Edited by E. Thomas. 2 Vols. (1858.) [S.]

RAM RAZ :—
(xxxi.) The Architecture of the Hindus. (1834.)

RODGERS, C. J. :—
(xxxii.) Catalogue of Coins in Government Museum, Lahore, published by Punjab Government. (Calcutta Baptist Mission Press, 1891.)
(xxxiii.) Catalogue of Coins in the Indian Museum. (Several parts.) (1894.)
(xxxiv.) Coin Collecting in Northern India. (Allahabad Pioneer Press, 1894.)

SMITH, V. A. :—
(xxxv.) Catalogue of the Hindu Coins in the Calcutta Museum. (Oxford, 1907.)

THOMAS E. :—
(xxxvi.) Chronicles of the Pathan Kings of Delhi. (1871.)

WARREN, J. :—
(xxxvii.) Kala Sankalita. (Indian eras and their reckoning.) (Madras, 1825.)

WARREN, S. J.:—
(xxxviii.) Two bas-reliefs of the Stupa of Bharhut. (Leiden.)

WEBB, H.:—
(xxxix.) The Currencies of the Hindu States of Rajputana. (Constable.) (1893.)

WRIGHT, H. N.:—
(xl.) Catalogue of the Muhammadan Coins in the Calcutta Museum. (Oxford, 1907.)

WILSON, H. H.:—
(xli.) Ariana Antiqua. (1841.) [**R.**]

PAPERS.

BANURJI, R,:—
(i.) The Kaimur Range. (Legends.) J. A. B., xlvi. (i.), 16.

BARNES, E.:—
(ii.) Dhār and Māndu. J. B. R. A. S., xxi., 339, 381, 417.

BENNETT J.:—
(iii.) The Bhar Kings of Eastern Oudh. I. A., i., 265.

BHANDARKAR, D. R.:—
(iv.) Epigraphic Notes. J. B. R. A. S., xxi., 392.

BHANDARKAR, R. G.:—
(v.) The Epoch of the Gupta Era. J. B. R. A. S., xvii., 80.
(vi.) The Work done by the Society towards the elucidation of Indian History, &c. J. B. R. A. S. Centenary Memorial, Vol. 33.

BROWN, R.:—
(vii.) The Mughal Mints in India. Num. Chr., 1903, 194.

BÜHLER, G.:—
(viii.) On the origin of the Gupta-Valabhi Era. W. Z. K. M., v., 215.
(ix.) The Inscriptions on the Sānchi Stupas. W. Z. K. M., vii., 291. (Also in Ep. Ind., ii., 87, 366.)
(x.) The Dabhoi Plates. Ep. Ind., i., 20.
(xi.) The Udepur Prasasti of the Kings of Mālava. Ep. In., i., 222.
(xii.) The new Inscription of Toramāna. Ep. Ind., i., 238.
(xiii.) The Cintra Prasasti. Ep. In., i., 271.
(xiv.) The Vadnagar Prasasti of the Reign of Kumārapala. Ep. Ind., i., 296.
(xv.) Votive inscriptions from the Sānchi Stupas. Ep. Ind., ii, 87, 366.
(xvi.) The Saka and Samvat Eras. I. A., vii., 180.
(xvii.) The Dohad Inscription of Jayasimha. I. A., x., 158.
(xviii.) Dates of the Vaghela Kings of Gujarāt. I. A., xxi., 276.

BURGESS, J.:—
(xix.) Sketch of Archæological Research in India during half a Century. J. B. R. A. S., Centenary Memorial, Vol. 131.
(xx.) The Inscriptions on the Sānchi Stupas. Academy, xliii., 526.

(xxi.) The Great Stupa of Sānchi-Kanakheda. J. R. A. S., 1902, 29.

(xxii.) Archæological Research in India. Actes VIII. Conge. Orient. Sect. Ary., i., 1 to 48.

BURN, R. :—

(xxiii.) The Bajranggarh mint. J. A .B., lxvi. (i.), 275.

(xxiv.) Mints of the Mughal emperors. J. A. B., lxxiii. (i.), 75.

(xxv.) Molapo. J. R. A. S., 1905, 837.

CAMPBELL, J. M. :—

(xxvi.) Māndu. J. B. R. A. S., xix., 154.

CARNEGY, J. :—

(xxvii.) The Bhars of Oudh and Benares. J. A. B., xlv. (i.), 297.

CARTELLIERI, F. :—

(xxviii.) Semra plates of Paramārdideva. Ep. In., iv., 153.

CHAKRAVARTI :—

(xxix.) Rāma tankis. J. A. B., lxi. (i.), 104.

(xxx.) Kalidāsa. J. R. A. S., 1903, 184.

CONOLLY, E. :—

(xxxi.) Observations upon the past and present condition of Ougein. J. A. B., vi., 813.

COPE, J. :—

(xxxii.) The remains at Ranod (Narod). J. A. B., xvi., 1079.

COTTON, J. S. :—

(xxxiii.) Indian Numismatics. Academy, xliv., 258.

COVERNTON, J. G. :—

(xxxiv.) Mālwa coins of Bahadur Shāh of Guzerat. N. Ch., 1903, 314.

CUNNINGHAM, SIR A. :—

(xxxv.) Coins of the Indo-Scythians. Num. Chr., 1888, 199.

(xxxvi.) The days of the week in India. I. A., xiv., 1.

(xxxvii.) The inscriptions of Toramāna Shāha. Academy, 15th Nov. 1890, 453.

(xxxviii.) The Pehoa Inscription (Kanauj). J. A. B., xxxiii., 223.

(xxxix.) Coins of the Sakas. Num. Chr., 1890, 103.

(xl.) The later Indo-Scythians. Num. Chr., III. Ser., Vol. XIII., 95, 166.

CUNNINGHAM, J. D. :—

(xli.) The antiquities of Bhopāl. J. A. B., xvi., 739.

(xlii.) On the ruins of Pathāri (Bhopāl). J. A. B., xvii., 305.

DANGERFIELD, F. :—

(xliii.) Some account of the caves near Baug. J. B. R. A. S., ii., 206.

DELMERICK, K. :—

(xliv.) A list of rare Muhammedan coins (Malwa). J. A. B., xlv., 291.

DROUIN, E. :—

(xlv.) The numbers and signs of deification on the coins of the Indo-Scythian Kings. I. A., xxii., 427.

(xlvi.) Les Monnais Touraniennes. Revue Numismatique. 1891.

FLEET, J. F.:—
(xlvii.) Srāvana Belgola Inscription of Prabha-Chandra. Ep. In., iv., 22.
(xlviii.) A Rashtrakuta inscription. I. A., xii., 214.
(xlix.) An inscription at Udayāgiri in Gwalior State. I. A., xiii., 185.
(l.) The Mandasor inscriptions. I. A., xv., 194, 222, 253.
(li.) The epoch of the Gupta era. I. A., xv., 189; xvi., 141, 418, 432; xvii., 359, xx., 376.
(lii.) The date of Mihirakula. I. A., xv., 245.
(liii.) The Bhopal plates of Udayāvarman. I. A., xvi., 252.
(liv.) The Saka Era. I. A., xvii., 205.
(lv.) The Chedi Era. I. A., xvii., 215.
(lvi.) The calculation of Hindu dates. I. A., xvi., 42, 74, 109, 197; xvii., 23, 141, 210, 239, 264 297; xviii., 30, 55, 90, 127, 285, 316, 379; xix., 41, 70, 102, 129, 155, 187, 317, 440; xx., 35, 191.
(lvii.) Grant of Ajayapāla. I. A., xviii., 80.
(lviii.) The Chedi Kings. I. A., xviii., 209.
(lix.) Toramāna and the Guptas in Central India. I. A., xviii., 225.
(lx.) The Bhitari seal of Kumāra Gupta. I. A., xix., 224.
(lxi.) The Chronology of the Eastern Chālukya Kings. Ind. Ant. xx., 1, 93, 266.
(lxii.) Bhadra Bahu and Chandra Gupta. I. A., xxi., 156.
(lxiii.) Hiuen Tsiang's Capital of Mahārāshtra. I. A., xxii., 113.
(lxiv.) A topographical list of the Brihat Sanhita. I. A., xxii., 169.
(lxv.) Some dates of the Chalukya Vikrama Kala. I. A., xxii., 296.
(lxvi.) The Gupta Inscriptions. C. I. I., Vol. III., pp. 21, 29, 34, 88, 93, 100, 106, 110, 112, 121, 132, 139, 159, 161, 231, 233, 259, 260, 279.
(lxvii.) A note on . . . the Gupta Era. J. B. R. A. S., xviii., 71.
(lxviii.) The Mandasor Inscription (a controversial letter). J. R. A. S., 1893, 396.
(lxix.) The conquests of Samudra Gupta. J. R. A. S., 1898, 369.
(lxx.) A hitherto unrecognised Kushān King. J. R. A. S., 1903, 325
(lxxi.) The date of Buddha's death. J. R. A. S., 1904, 1.
(lxxii.) Vasashka, Vasushka. J. R. A. S., 1905, 357.
(lxxiii.) Trikuta and the so-called Kalachuri or Chedi Era. J. R. A. S., 1905, 566.
(lxxiv.) The traditional date of Kanishka. J. R. A. S., 1906, 979.

GRIERSON, G. A.:—
(lxxv.) The Vikrama Samvat. Athenæum, 1888, 72.
(lxxvi.) Yuan Chwang's Molapo. J. R. A. S., 1906, 95.

HALL, FITZ E.:—
(lxxvii.) Two land grants (Rāshtrakūta). J. A. B., xxvii., 217.
(lxxviii.) Two plates of M. R. Hastīn from Nāgod. J. A. B., xxx., 7.

(lxxix.) An Inscription of Vākpati of Dhār. J. A. B., xxx., 195.
(lxxx.) The Harsauda inscription. J. A. B., xxviii., 1.
(lxxxi.) Vestiges of the Royal lines of Kanyākubja. J. A. B., xxxi., 1.
(lxxxii.) Three Sanskrit inscriptions. J. A. B., xxxi., 111.
(lxxxiii.) Vestiges of the Kings of Gwalior. J. A. B., xxxi., 391.
(lxxxiv.) The Berāghāt inscription. J. A. O. S., vi., 499.
(lxxxv.) Grant of Vairasimhadeva (Kachhapagata). J.A.O.S., vi., 538.
(lxxxvi.) The Mandala Kings. J. A. O. S., vii, 12.
(lxxxvii.) Two Paramāra records. J. A. O. S., vii., 24. (*See also* J. A. B., ix., 545.)

HAY, J :—
(lxxxviii.) The Turan Mall hill. J. A. B., xx., 502.

HIRTH, J. :—
(lxxxix.) Chao Jukna's Ethnography (Malwa). J. R. A. S., 1896, 477, 488.

HOERNLE, A. F. :—
(xc.) Eight gold Gupta coins. Pr: J. A. B., 1891, 117.
(xci.) Rāmtinkis. Pr: J. A. B., 1893, 156.
(xcii.) Two gold Gupta coins. Pr: J. A. B., 1893, 95.
(xciii.) Rare Hindu and Muhammedan coins. J. B. A., lviii. (i.), 30; lxix. (i.), 69.
(xciv.) The seal of Kumāra-Gupta. J. A. B., lviii. (i.), 85.
(xcv.) Some problems of Indian history. J. R. A. S., 1903, 545; 1905, 1.
(xcvi.) Rock cut inscription from Riwa. I. A., ix., 120.
(xcvii.) Readings from the Bharhut Stupa. I. A., x., 118, 255; xi., 25. (*See ibid*, 47.)
(xcviii.) Notes on coins of Native States. J. A. B., lxvi. (i.), 261.
(xcix.) Copper coins of the Suri dynasty. J. A. B., lix. (i.), 154.
(c.) Silver seal of Kumāra Gupta. Pr: J. A. B. 1889, 194.

HULTZSCH :—
(ci.) Two inscriptions on the Vaillabhattasvāmin temple at Gwalior. Ep. In., i., 154.
(cii.) The Mahoba inscription. Ep. In., i., 217.
(ciii.) Two inscriptions from Gwalior. Ep. Ind., iv., 161.
(civ.) Dhār prasasti of Arjunavarman. Ep. In., viii., 96.
(cv.) Inscriptions on the Barhut Stupa. I. A., xiv., 138.
(cvi.) The Gwalior inscription of V. S., 1161. I. A., xv., 201.
(cvii.) Bharaut inscriptions. I. A., xxi., 225.

IMPEY, DR. :—
(cviii.) The Kholvee caves. J. A. B., v., 336.
(cix.) Description of a collossal Jain figure at Barwāni. J. A. B., xviii., 918.
(cx.) The Bāgh caves. J. B. R. A. S., v., i.
(cxi.) Inscriptions, Note on the copying of. I. A., ii., 183.

IRVINE, W. :—
(cxii.) Notes on some old Mughal mint towns. Pr: J. A. B., 1893, 18.

JACKSON, A. M. T. :—
(cxiii.) Summary of numismatic researches. J. B. R. A. S. Centenary Memorial, Vol. 407.

JACOBI, H. :—
(cxiv.) The computation of Hindu dates. Ep. Ind., i., 403.
(cxv.) Returns and Tables for verifying Hindu dates. I. A., xvii., 115.

JOHNSTON, C. :—
(cxvi.) The date of Vikramāditya. Academy, xliii., 374.

JOHNSTON, J. M. C. :—
(cxvii.) Mohammedan coins. Num. Chr., 1899, 265.

KEITH, J. :—
(cxviii.) Report on the fortress of Gwalior. (Calcutta, 1883).

KIELHORN, F. :—
(cxix.) Inscriptions at Khajrāho. Ep. Ind., i., 121.
(cxx.) The Siyadoni Inscription. Ep. Ind., i., 162.
(cxxi.) Two Chandella Inscriptions. Ep. Ind., i., 195.
(cxxii.) The Jhānsi Inscription. Ep. In., i., 214.
(cxxiii.) The Bilhari Stone Inscription. Ep. In., i., 251.
(cxxiv.) Harsauda stone inscriptions of Devapaladeva of Dhāra. Ep. Ind., i., 310.
(cxxv.) Two Chandella Inscriptions from Ajaygadh. Ep. Ind., i., 325.
(cxxvi.) Stone inscription from Ranod (Narod). Ep. In., i., 351.
(cxxvii.) Jabalpur copper plate inscriptions of Yasahakarnadeva. (A.D. 1122). Ep. Ind., ii., 3.
(cxxviii.) Bheraghāt stone inscriptions of the Queen Alhanadevi, of the Chedi year 907. Ep. Ind., ii., 7.
(cxxix.) Tewar stone inscription of the reign of Jāyasimhadeva, of the Chedi year 928. Ep. Ind., ii., 17–19.
(cxxx.) Karitalai Stone Inscriptions of the Reign of the Chedi Lakshmanarāja. Ep. Ind., ii., 174.
(cxxxi.) The Nāgpur Prasasti of the Rulers of Mālava. Ep. In., ii., 180.
(cxxxii.) The Dubkund Inscription. Ep. In., ii., 232.
(cxxxiii.) Benares Copper Plates of Karnadeva Chedi. Ep. Ind., ii., 297.
(cxxxiv.) Mandhāta Plates of Jaya Sinha. Ep. In., iii., 46.
(cxxxv.) Bahal Inscription of Singhana. Ep. In., iii., 110.
(cxxxvi.) A list of the inscriptions of Northern India. Ep. In., v. (Appendix).
(cxxxvii.) Kahla Plates of Sodhadeva Chedi. Ep. In., vii., 85.
(cxxxviii.) Grant of Bhojadeva of Mahodaya. Ep. In., vii., 208.
(cxxxix.) A list of inscriptions of Southern India. Ep. In., viii. (Appendix.)
(cxl.) Supplement to list of inscriptions of Northern India. E. In., viii. (Appendix.)
(cxli.) *Ib.* of Southern India. Ep. In., viii. (Appendix II).
(cxlii.) Grant of Vākpati of Dhāra. I. A., xiv., 159.
(cxliii.) The Sās-bāhu Inscription at Gwalior. I. A., xv., 33.
(cxliv.) Three Chandella copper plate grants. I. A., xvi., 201.

(cxlv.) The Terahi inscriptions. I. A., xvii., 201.
(cxlvi.) Four Rewah copper plates. I. A., xvii., 224.
(cxlvii.) Two Chandella Inscriptions. I. A., xviii., 237.
(cxlviii.) The Vikrama Era. I. A., xviii., 251.
(cxlix.) Three Inscriptions at Udaypur in Gwalior. I. A., xviii., 341.
(cl.) The Kanasva Grant. I. A., xix., 55.
(cli.) Examination of Questions connected with the Vikrama Era. I. A., xix., 20, 166, 354; xx., 124, 397.
(clii.) Visaladeva's Inscription on Firoz Shāh's Lāt. I. A., xix., 215.
(cliii.) The Mālava Era. I. A., xix., 316.
(cliv.) Three Ujjain copper plate grants. I. A., xix., 345.
(clv.) The Udayāpura Inscriptions. I. A., xx., 83.
(clvi.) A note on the Saptarshi Era. Ind. Ant., xx., 149.
(clvii.) Sanskrit. plays partly preserved as inscriptions at Ajmere. I. A., xx., 201.
(clviii.) Grant of Devapāladeva of Dhār. I. A., xx., 310.
(clix.) Mungir copper plate grant of Devapalādeva. I. A., xxi., 253.
(clx.) Six unpublished Inscriptions of Narwar Kings and Guhila Kings. I. A., xxii., 80.
(clxi.) On the Dates of the Saka Era in Inscriptions. I. A., xxiii., 113.
(clxii.) The Ichāwar Grants of Paramārdideva. I. A., xxv., 205.
(clxiii.) Dates in the Harsha Era. I. A., xxvi., 29.
(clxiv.) Festal days of the Hindu Lunar Calendar, I. A., xxvi., 177.
(clxv.) Sanskrit Plays preserved as Inscriptions. Academy, Jan. 1891, 67.
(clxvi.) The Initial Point of the Chedi Era. Göttingen Nachrichten, 1888, 31.
(clxvii.) The Pathāri pillar inscription. Göttingen Nachrichten, 1901, 519.
(clxviii.) Bijapur Inscription of Dhavala of Hastikundi. J. A. B., lxii. (i.), 309.
(clxix.) The Epoch of the Kalachuri Era. Transactions of the Oriental Congress of 1892. i., 428.
(clxx.) A Note on Prof. Bühler's Paper on the Origin of the Gupta Valabhi Era. W. Z. K. M., vi., 107.

KHAN ALI :—
(clxxi.) Account of a March between Mhow and Saugor. J. A. B., viii., 805; ix., 311.

KINCAID, COL. :—
(clxxii.) Rambles in Central India (the Bhojpur Lake). I. A., xvii., 348.

KING, L. W. :—
(clxxiii.) History and Coinage of Mālwā. N. Chr. (1904), 62, ff.

KING, L. W. and VOST :—
(clxxiv.) Novelties in Mughal coins. N. Chr., xvi. (1895), 155.

KIRTANE, N. J.:—
(clxxv.) Three Mālwā Inscriptions. I. A., vi., 48.

LEVI, S.:—
(clxxvi.) Sur quelques termes employés dans les Inscriptions des Kshatrapas. J. A., xix., 95.
(clxxvii.) Notes on the Indo-Scythians. I. A., xxxiii., 110.

LUARD, C. E.:—
(clxxviii.) The Buddhist Caves of Mālwā. I. A., 1908.
(clxxix.) The Mandasor Pillar. I. A., 1908.
(clxxx.) The Bhojpur Lake and Temples. I. A., 1908.

MAISEY, LT.:—
(clxxxi.) The Antiquities of Kālinjār. J. A. B., xvii., 171, 313.

MITRA, R. L.:—
(clxxxii.) The so-called Dasyus of Sānchi. I. A., i., 36.
(clxxxiii.) Bhoja of Dhār and his Homonyms. J. A. B., xxxii., 91.
(clxxxiv.) Copper Plates from Bānda (Chandella). J. A. B., xlvii., 74, 80.

MÜLLER, MAX:—
(clxxxv.) The Vikramāditya Era. I. A., xii., 230.

NASIK INSCRIPTIONS:—
(clxxxvi.) Nāsik Inscriptions. *See* Arch. Surv. Reports for Western India, ii, 128; iii., 82, 134; iv., 98.

PHOTOGRAPHIC NEGATIVES:—
(clxxxvii.) Photographic Negatives of Antiquities, A list of. (Supt. Govt. Printing, Calcutta.) Rs. 4.

RICE, L.:—
(clxxxviii.) Bhadra Bāhu and Srāvana Belgola. I. A., iii., 153.

RAPSON, E. J.:—
(clxxxix.) The Coinage of the Mahā Kshatrapas . . . . of Malwa. J. R. A. S. 1899, 357.
(cxc.) Notes on Indian Coins and Seals. J. R. A. S., 1900, 97, 423, 529; 1901 97.
(cxci.) Notes on Indian Coins and Seals. J. R. A. S., 1903, 285.
(cxcii.) Notes on Indian Coins and Seals. J. R. A. S., 1905, 783.

RODGERS, C. J.:—
(cxciii.) Coins supplementary to Thomas' Chronicles of the Pathan Kings. J. A. B., lxiii. (i)., 63.
(cxciv.) Jahāngīr's Mohurs and Rupees. Pr: J. A. B., 1894, 90.
(cxcv.) A General Review of the Coinage of the Mogul Emperors of India. Cal. Rev., xlix., 126.
(cxcvi.) Rupees of the Suri Dynasty. I. A., xvii., 64.

SCHRAM, R.:—
(cxcvii.) Tables for the Conversion of Hindu dates. I. A., xviii., 290.

SCOTT, H. R.:—
(cxcviii.) Description of a hoard of 1,200 Kshatrapa coins. J. B. R. A. S., xx., 201.

SENART, E. :—
(cxcix.) The Inscriptions in the Caves at Nāsik. Ep. In., viii., 59.

SINCLAIR, J. :—
(cc.) Rough Notes on Khandesh. The Mānbhavas. I. A., iv., 335.

SMITH, V. A. :—
(cci.) Græco-Roman influence on the Civilisation of Ancient India. J. A. B., lviii. (i.), 107; lxi. (i.), 50; lxii. (i.), 84; Pr: 1889, 209.
(ccii.) Coins of Sallakshana Pāla Deva, Madana Pāla Deva, and Prithivi Deva. Pr: J. A. B., 1890, 205.
(cciii.) Notes on the Bhars. J. A. B., xlvi. (i.), 227.
(cciv.) Buddhist Statuette and Chandella copper plate. J. A. B., lxiv. (i.), 155.
(ccv.) Observations on the Gupta Coinage. J. R. A. S., 1893, 77.
(ccvi.) Kausāmbi. J. R. A. S., 1898, 503.
(ccvii.) The Iron Pillar at Dhār. J. R. A. S., 1898, 143.
(ccviii.) The Identity of Piyadasi with Asoka Maurya. J. R. A. S., 1901, 827.
(ccix.) The Kushān or Indo-Scythian Period of Indian History. J. R. A. S., 1903, 1.
(ccx.) The Position of the Autonymous Tribes conquered by Alexander the Great. J. R. A. S., 1903, 685.
(ccxi.) The Coinage of the Early or Imperial Gupta dynasty. J. R. A. S., xxi., 1.
(ccxii.) Asoka Notes. I. A., xxxii., 364; xxxiv., 200, 245.
(ccxiii.) The Indian King named Silāditya and the Kingdom of Mo-la-po. Z. D. M. G., lviii., 787.
(ccxiv.) Indian Numismatics. Academy. October 31. 388.
(ccxv.) Note on the Progress of Indian Numismatics. As. Qu. Rev. ii. (Series V.), 10, p. 370.
(ccxvi.) Andhra History and Coinage. Z. D. M. G., lvi., 649; lvii., 605.

SPECHT, E. :—
(ccxvii.) Du déchiffrement des monnaies Sindo-Ephthalites, J. A. (Series IX.), xvii., 487.
(ccxviii.) Etudes sur l'Asie centrale. J. A., 1883, ii.

TAYLOR, G. :—
(ccxix.) The Coins of the Gujarāt Sultanāt. J. B. R. A. S., xxi., 278.
(ccxx.) The Mints of the Mughal Emperors of India. J. B. R. A. S., Centenary Memorial, Vol. 411.

THEOBALD, W. :—
(ccxxi.) Notes on some of the Symbols found on the Punch-marked Coins of Hindustān, and on their Relationship to the Archaic Symbolism of other Races. J. A. B., lix., 181.
(ccxxii.) A Revision of the Symbols on the Karshapana Coinage. J. A. B., lxx., 38.

TULLA, VASUDEVA :—
(ccxxiii.) Maheshvara in Malwā. I. A., iv., 246.

UJJAIN :—
(ccxxiv.) A Note on Coins from (with Plate). J. A. B., vii., 1054.

VOGEL, J. PH. :—
(ccxxv.) Epigraphical discoveries at Sarnath. Ep. Ind., viii., 166.

VOST, W. :—
(ccxxvi.) Kausāmbi. J. R. A. S., 1904, 249.

WILKINSON, L. :—
(ccxxvii.) Grants from Bhopal (Piplianagar) of the Paramāras. J. A. B., v., 377; vii., 736.

SECTION V.

LANGUAGE, LITERATURE, ARTS, &c.

BOOKS AND PAPERS.

BEAMES, J. :—
(i.) Comparative Grammar. 3 Vols. (1879).

BHANDARKAR, S. R. :—
(ii.) Report of the preliminary tour through Central India, in search of Sanskrit MSS. (1904.)

BHANDARKAR, J. R. :—
(iii.) On the search for Sanskrit MSS. in the Bombay circle. &c., J. B. R. A. S. Mem. Vol. 58.
(iv.) Separate Reports on the search for Sanskrit MSS. (Several issues.)

CUST, R. N. :—
(v.) Linguistic and Oriental Essays written from 1840 to 1901. (Luzac, 1901.)

GRIERSON, G. A. :—
(vi.) Languages in India. J. R. A. S., 1903, 425.
(vii.) Streams of Immigration. J. A. O. S., xxiii., 361.
(viii.) Linguistic Survey of India. Rajputana, Central India, and Ajmere-Merwara. (1899), II., III.
(ix.) On the East Central Group of Indo-Aryan Vernaculars. I. A., xxviii., 262.
(x.) The modern Indo-Aryan Alphabets. J. R. A. S. 1904, 67.

GRUNWEDEL, A. :—
(xi.) Buddhist Art in India, translated by J. Burgess and Agnes Gibson. (Quaritch.) (1901.)

FALLON :—
(xii.) Dictionary, Hindusthani-English (containing Proverbs, &c.) (Calcutta, 1858.)

HOERNLE, F. A. :—
(xiii.) Comparative Grammar of the Gaudian Languages (Eastern Hindi). (1880.)

HOPKINS, W. :—
(xiv.) Indian literature. Hill & Co. (New York, 1897.)

KELLOG, S. H. :—
(xv.) A Grammar of the Hindi Language. (Kegan Paul Trench.) (1893.)

LEECH, MAJ. R. :—
(xvi.) Notes on a Short Vocabulary of the dialectof Bundelkhand. J. A. B., xii., 1086.

MACDONELL, A. A. :—
(xvii.) A History of Sanskrit Literature. (Heinemann.) (1900.)

MOLESWORTH, J. T. :—
(xviii.) Marathi Dictionary (M.–E. and E.–M.) (Bombay, 1831.)

PETERSON, J. :—
(xix.) Reports on Search for Sanskrit MSS. Four issues. (Bombay, 1884–94.)

PINCOTT, F. :—
(xx.) The Hindi Manual.

SLEEMAN, COL. W. H. :—
(xxi.) Ramaseena. (Calcutta, 1836.)

WEBER, A. :—
(xxii.) The History of Indian Literature. (1878.)
(xxiii.) Sacred Literature of the Jains. Translated by Hubert Weir-Smyth. I. A. xxi., 177–85 ; 210–5 ; 293–311 ; 327–41 ; 369–73. 36.

WILSON, H. H. :—
(xxiv.) The Theatre of the Hindus. 2 Vols. (1871.)

SECTION VI.

SCIENTIFIC (NATURAL HISTORY, BOTANY &c.).

BOOKS AND PAPERS.

BAILLY, H.:—
(i.) Traite de l'Astronomie Indienne. (Paris, 1787.)

BARNES, H. E.:—
(ii.) The Birds of the Bombay Presidency. (Calcutta, 1885.)

BEDDOME, R. H.:—
(iii.) Flora Sylvatica. 3 Vols. (Madras, 1873.)

BEAVAN, R.:—
(iv.) The Freshwater Fishes of India. (1877.)

BLANFORD, W. T.:—
(v.) The Fauna of British India. 15 Vols. (Taylor and Francis. (1888 to 1902.)
(vi.) The Reptilia and Amphibia of Central India. J. A. B., xxxix. (ii.), 335.

BLANFORD, H. F.:—
(vii.) The Climate and Weather of India. (1889.)

BOULENGER, G. A.:—
(viii.) The Reptilia and Batrachia of British India. (1890.)

BRANDIS, D.:—
(ix.) Indian Trees. (1906.)
(x.) The Forest Flora of North-Western and Central India. 2 Vols. (1874.)

BURGESS, E.:—
(xi.) The Surya Siddhanta. J. A. O. S., vi., 141.

BURGESS, J.:—
(xii.) Notes on Hindu Astronomy. (Hertford, 1893.)
(xiii.) Notes on Hindu Astronomy. J. R. A. S., 1893, 717 (same as above).

DAY, F.:—
(xiv.) The Fishes of India. 2 Vols. (1878.)

DEWAR, D.:—
(xv.) Bombay Ducks (Ornithology). (1906.)

DRURY, H.:—
(xvi.) The Useful Plants of India. (1873.)

EDGWORTH, J.:—
(xvii.) A Catalogue of the Plants found in the Banda District. J. A. B., xxii., 24.

FAYRER, SIR J.:—
(xviii.) The Thanatophidia of India. (1872.)

FLEET, J. F.:—
(xix.) A Table of the Intercalary and Expunged Months of the Hindu Calendar. I. A., xxiii., 104.

GAMBLE, J. S.:—
(xx.) A Manual of Indian Timbers. (1902.)

(xxi.) GEOLOGY:—
See Gazetteers. *Also* Geology of the Vindhyan Series. Memoirs of the Geological Survey of India, vii., 1.
Geology of Gwalior and the vicinity. Records of the Geological Survey of India, iii., 33; xxx., 16. Memoirs of the Geological Survey of India, vi., Part 3.
Geology of the Son Valley. Memoirs of the Geological Survey of India, xxxi., Part 1.
Southern Coalfields of the Rewah and Gondwana Basin. Memoir of the Geological Survey of India, xxxi., 3.
Cretaceous Beds of Bagh and the Lametas. Quarterly Journal of the Geological Society., xxx.; Records of the Geological Survey of India, xx., 81.
Mica Deposits of India. Memoir of the Geological Survey of India, xxxiv., 11, 121.
Geology of the State of Panna (Diamond Mines). Records of the Geographical Survey of India, xxxiii., Part IV., 262.
Fossil Flora of the Gondwana System, by Feistmantel and Zeiller in the *Paleontologica Indica.*
The Ammonites of the Bâgh Beds. E. Vredenburg. Records of the Geological Survey of India, xxxvi., Part II., 109.

HOOKER, SIR J. D.:—
(xxii.) Flora of British India. 7 Vols. (Reeve & Co.) (1875–98.)
(xxiii.) A Sketch of the Flora of British India. (1904.)

HUME and MARSHALL:—
(xxiv.) The Game Birds of India, Burma, and Ceylon. 3 Vols. (1879.)

HUNTER, J.:—
(xxv.) Some Account of the Astronomical Labours of Jayasinha. (Deals with Jai Singh's Observatory at Ujjain.) Asíatic Researches, v., 194.

JERDON:—
(xxvi.) The reptiles of Peninsular India. J. A. B., xxii., 462, 522.
(xxvii.) The birds of India. 3 Vols. (Calcutta, 1877.)
(xxviii.) The mammals of India. (1874.)

KANYA LAL:—
(xxix.) Forest flora of the Dehra Dun Circle. (Calcutta, 1901.)

KING, W.:—
(xxx.) The birds of the Goona district. J. A. B., xxxviii., 208.

MARSHALL, G. C. J.:—
(xxxi.) Bird nesting in India (a calendar). (Calcutta, 1877.)

MEDLICOTT, H. B., BLANFORD, W. T., BALL, V.:—
(xxxii.) Manual of the Geology of India. 3 Vols. Edited by R. D. Oldham (third volume, Economic Geology.) (Calcutta, 1893.)

LE MESSURIER, COL. A.:—
(xxxiii.) The game, shore, and water birds of India. (Calcutta, 1888.)

MURRAY, J. A.:—
(xxxiv.) The Avifauna of British India. 2 Vols. (Bombay, 1890.)

NAIRNE, A. K.:—
(xxxv.) The flowering plants of Western India. (Allen.) (1894).

OATES, E. W.:—
(xxxvi.) The game birds of India. 2 Vols. (1899.)

OLIVER, D.:—
(xxxvii.) First book of Indian Botany. (1869.)

SCHLAGINTWEIT:—
(xxxviii.) An Enumeration of the Hot Springs of India. J. A. B., xxxiii., 49.

STERNDALE, R. A.:—
(xxxix.) Seonnee, or Life on the Satpura Range. (1877.)
(xl.) Mammalia of India. (1887.)

SURVEY:—
(xli.) Cadastral. *See* Gazetteer (Survey commenced 1861).

TALBOT, W. A.:—
(xlii.) The Trees and Shrubs and Woody Climbers of the Bombay Presidency. (Bombay, 1894.)

THOMAS, E.:—
(xliii.) On Ancient Indian Weights. J. A. B., xxiii., 251; xxiv., 14, 52.

WATT, G.;—
(xliv.) A Dictionary of the Economic Products of India. 6 Vols. 1889–93.

WHITNEY, W. D.:—
(xlv.) Hindu and Chinese system of Asterisms. J. A. O. S., viii., 1.

WIGHT, R.:—
(xlvi.) Icones Plantarum Indiae Orientalis. 6 Vols. (Madras, 1840–45.)

CHRONOLOGICAL TABLES OF CENTRAL INDIA HISTORY.

NOTE.

This Chronology gives all the important dates in the history of Central India which are known to me.

In the early history and up to 1527, Miss Duff's admirable "Chronology" has been largely referred to, such alterations being made in the dates and references there given as later investigations seem to warrant.

The tables have been arranged in accordance with the four periods into which the history naturally divides itself.

The "Early Period" comprises two sections, the one witnessing the spread of Buddhism under Asoka and its decay, and the other the rise and fall of the great empire of Harshavardhana, terminating with the formation of numerous petty principalities (270 B.C. to 700 A.D.).

The "Muhammadan Period" also falls into two sections. The first saw the subjugation of the Rājput principalities by the early Muhammadan dynasties of Delhi (970 to 1527 A.D.) ; the second the formation of the Mughal Empire and its decay at the death of Aurangzeb, when the shadow of the approaching Marāthā conquest was already falling across Mālwā (1527 to 1707 A.D.)

The "Marāthā Period" (1707 to 1818 A.D.), one of incessant civil strife and turmoil, saw the sway of the Peshwas firmly established in Central India, and finally its substitution by the independent rule of the houses of Sindhia, Holkar and the Ponwār. The last 20 years witnessed the gradual establishment of British supremacy and the suppression of disorder by the wars of 1803–05 and 1817.

The "Modern Period" is one of reconstruction, and although, save for the severe upheaval of 1857, less rich than the preceding periods in historical incidents, is no wit less important.

It should be remarked that only the most important references are given here, and that the Index must be consulted for fuller information.

C. E. L.

CHRONOLOGICAL TABLES OF CENTRAL INDIA HISTORY.

[N.B.—*V. Sam.*=*Vikrama Samvat*. *G.E.*=*Gupta Era*. *H*=*Higri*. *S*=*Saka Era*].

A. Early Period (Circ. 600 B.C. to 970 A.D.)

B.C.

3102 Friday, February 18th. Date of the commencement of the Kaliyuga of the Hindus. It precedes the Vikrama Samvat by 3044 years and the Saka Era by 3179 years.

570 Siddhārtha afterwards Gautama Buddha born at Kapilvastu.

490 Death of Mahāvira the last of the Jain Tirthankars.—*The Indian sect of Jainas*, by G. Bühler.

487 Buddha's death.—*Early History*, 40. I. A., ii., 139. J. R. A. S. 1903, 289; 1904, 355.

327–23 Alexander's invasion.—*Early History*, 42–106 (where all references will be found).

321 Chandragupta establishes the Maurya dynasty at Pātaliputra.—*Early History*, 108–172 (all references are given). Chandragupta was the Sandrokotos of the Greek writers.

297 Bindusāra Maurya succeeds his father, Chandragupta. By the Greeks he is known as Amitrochates *i.e.* Amitraghāta "the destroyer of enemies."—*Early History*, 129.

272 Asoka succeeded his father Bindusāra at Pātaliputra.—*Early History*, 135. *Asoka, the Buddhist*, by V. A. Smith. (Clarendon Press). Fleet, J. R. A. S., 1908, 471.

269 Formal Abhisheka or anointing of Asoka at Pātaliputra. The year 257 B.C. in which, according to Bühler, the Rupnāth and Sahasrām edicts are dated, corresponds to the last of his reign. The chief events mentioned in his edicts are:—In his 13th year (259) he instituted annual tours throughout his dominions in search of religious truth; and in his 15th and 16th (257–256) issued a series of 14 rock-cut Edicts laying down rules for guidance in religious matters and for the propagation of the Dhamma or sacred law by his officials on their annual tours through their districts also appointing *Dhammamahāmātras* or Superintendents of the sacred law. Under Asoka the Mauryan Empire extended over the whole of Northern India from Afghānistān to Mysore and from Kāthiāwār to Kālinga (Orissa).

B.C.

250 Erection of the *stūpas* at Bhārhut and Sānchi.—*See* Index s.v. Bharhut and Sānchī.

232–231 Asoka died. He was succeeded by Dasaratha his grandson, and the Maurya Empire fell to pieces soon after.

220 The Andhra dynasty rises to power soon after the death of Asoka under a ruler called Simuka.—*See* B.C. 27.

184 Rise of the Andhrabhritya or Sātavāhana dynasty. Names of three of the early princes of this dynasty occur in inscriptions belonging to the first half of the second century B.C.

Pushyamitra overthrows the last of the Mauryas now a weak petty chieftain and founds the Sunga dynasty. Pātaliputra continued the capital and all the central districts were held by him, but the more distant provinces broke away from their allegiance. Eastern Mâlwā, however, still formed part of his dominions, his son Agnimitra being Viceroy with headquarters at Vidisa, the modern Bhīlsa. An inscription on one of the gates of the Bhārut *stūpa* refers to their rule.—I. A., xxi., 225.

148 Agnimitra succeeds his father. He is the hero of Kālidāsa's play *Mālavikāgnimitra.* Pushyamitra carried out the *Asvamedha* or horse sacrifice, and thus marked the revival of Brāhmanism.—W. V. P., iv., 190. *Mālavikāgnimitra*, edited by Shankar Pandit. W. H. T., ii., 345. I. A., i., 301; ii., 61, 362; xiv., 138; xxi., 253. A. S. W. I., v., 73. Silvain Levi. *Theatre Indien*, 165. Cowell and Thomas. *Harshaçarita.*

63 Extinction of the Sunga dynasty by Vasudeva, who founds the Kānva line.

57 14th March, B.C. 57. Initial date of the Samvat Era, corresponding to the *Chaitra sudi*, 1st of the Kaliyuga year 3044 expired.

The year is luni-solar, but its initial element is determined by the *solar* year, and the Vikrama year thus commences with the new moon immediately preceding the first day of the *solar* month *Vaisākh*, when the sun enters *Mesha* (Aries). The initial date falls in March or April of our era. In Central India the months usually follow the *pūrnimānta*, reckoning from full moon to full moon, the year commencing on the *Chaitra sudi* 1*st*.—"Prinsep's Essays" (Thomas), ii., 154; I.A., vii., 180; xii., 230; xix., 316; xx., 405, 409; xxvi., 177; E.I., i., Part viii.; ii., 336.

27 The Andhras, who had risen to power on the death of Asoka, extend their dominion northward and destroy the Kānva dynasty. The Andhras then rose to great power, their dominions including the territory of the Sakas and Mālavas, and most of Gujarāt and Kāthiāwār, but in A.D. 100 the Western Kshatrapa Nahapāna deprived them of their possessions in Mālwā, which passed to the Kshatrapa's (*See* A.D. 100).—*Early History*, 183.

A.D.

78 Saturday, 14th March. The initial day of the Saka era, corresponding to 1*st sudi Chaitra*, Kaliyug 3179, expired. It is a sidereal year commencing with the sun's entry into Aries. Its first day coincides with the new moon of the *solar* month Chaitra. It was originally a dynastic era. Many inscriptions are dated in this era.—*See under* B.C. 57, and I. A., xvii., 205.

100 Rise of the Western Kshatrapa dynasty of Mālwā and Gujarāt. Nahapāna, the Ksharāta or Kshatrapa, extends his power over Mālwā and Gujarāt, driving out the Andhra King Vilivāyakura II. The Kshahrātas were apparently Sakas.—*Early History*, 188.

The Kushān dynasty (100–226) arose at this time, but has little concern with Central India.

126 Nahapāna was succeeded by Chashtana, who ruled from Ujjain, and is mentioned by Ptolemy (A.D. 150) as Tiastenos of Ozene. Chashtana's successors held Mālwā until 398, when they were overthrown by Chandra Gupta Vikramāditya.

138 Rudradāman the Kshatrapa, grandson of Chashtana succeeded. He married his daughter Dakshamitrā to the Andhra King Pulumāyi II. (the Siro Polemaios of Ptolemy). This did not curb his ambition, and he recovered much land from his son-in-law. An inscription of Rudradāman dated *Saka* 72 (A.D. 150) exists at Junāgarh. Coins of the Kshatrapas are found in Mālwā.—For Kshatrapas *see Early History*, 255. A. S. W. I., ii., 128, 140; iv., 101, 109. J. R. A. S., 1890, 639; 1899, 357. I. A., vii., 257; x., 157; xxi., 205. J. A., xix., 95.

249 Initial year of the Chedi, Kalachuri, or Haihaya era, which commenced on 28th July, 249, corresponding to *Bhadrapada sudi* 1st.—*Early History*, 307. I. A., xvii., 215.

308 Chandra Gupta I. rose from the feudatory position held by his grandfather Gupta and father Ghatotkacha to supreme power in Māgadha.

320 26th February to 13th March, 321 A.D. Initial date of the Gupta or Vallabhi era (G. E.) used on Gupta and Vallabhi inscriptions, coins, and grants.—I. A., xv., 189, 222, 278; xvii., 359; xxxi., 257; J. B. R. A. S., xvii., 2, 80. C. I. I., iii. *Introduction*.

326 Samudragupta, son of Chandragupta, succeeds his father. He had the "Allāhābād pillar" inscription incised, which records his victories. Among other conquests those over Ganpati Nāga, the ruler of Narwar, and over the "Kings of the forest country" in Baghelkhand are mentioned; while among the tribes on his frontier were the Mālavas of Mālwā, the Abhīras living in the country running down the east of the Mālwā plateau, from Gwalior to south of Jhānsi, still known as Ahīrwāra, and the Sakas, or western Kshatrapas of Mālwā.—*Early History*, 244. J. R. A. S., 1897, 859.

A.D.

375 Chandragupta II. succeeds his father, He took the name of Vikramāditya ("the sun of power") and is most probably the original king of Indian legend whose name is invariably connected with the Samvat era of Mālwā. He rapidly extended his possessions southward and westwards.

390 Chandragupta II. destroyed the Kshatrapa power in Mālwā, defeating and killing Rudrasinha, and by 398 the whole tract had passed into his power.—*See* references given under 138

399 Fa-hien, the Chinese pilgrim, visits India (399 to 414).—Beal, *Buddhist records of the Western World*; T. Legge, *Travels of Fa-hien.*

401 Inscription at Udayagiri of Chandragupta II. dated G. E. 82 = 401–02 A.D.—C. I. I., iii., 21.

An undated record of his also exists there.—*Ibid*, 34.

412 G. E. 93, Sānchī inscription.—C. I. I., iii., 29.

413 Kumāragupta I. succeeded Chandragupta.—*Early History*. C. I. I., iii., 39–45; J. R. A. S., xxi., 128.

422 Chedi Sam, 174, 177. Copper-plates from Kārītālai and Khoh in Bhagelkhand, issued by Jaynātha Mahārāja of Uchchakalpa, a chief who ruled in Bhagelkhand, and was a feudatory of the Guptas.—C. I. I., iii., 117, 121; I. A., xix., 227.

423 V. Sam, 480, Gangrār (Jhāllawār) inscription of Visvavarman of western Mālwā, successor of one Naravarman, apparently his father or elder brother.—C. I. I., iii., 72; J. B. A., lviii., (i), 100.

425 G. E., 106. Inscriptions from Jaina cave at Udayagiri.—C. A. S. R., x., 53; C. I. I., iii., 258.

437 V. Sam, 493. Mandasor inscription of Bandhuvarman, son of Visvavarman, and a feudatory of Kumāragupta I. The inscription records the building of a temple at Dasapura (Mandasor) in the time of these princes, and also its subsequent repair "under other kings," in V. Sam, 529 (473).—C. I. I., iii., 79; I. A., xvi., 194; xviii., 227, J. B. R. A. S., xvii., 80.

441 Chedi Sam, 193, 197, 214. Khoh copper-plates issued by Sarvanātha Mahārājā of Uchchalkalpa (in Baghelkhand), successor of Jaynātha, and contemporary with the local Parivrājaka chief, Hastin.—C. I. I., iii., 125, 135, and refs. under A.D. 422.

450 G. E., 131. Sānchī convent inscription.—C. I. I., iii, 261.

455 G. E., 136. Skandagupta of Māgadha, son and successor of Kumāragupta I. He restored the fallen fortunes of his family, and kept the rising power of the Hunas in check.

475 G. E., 156, 163, 191. Copper-plates from Khoh and Majhgawān, in Baghelkhand, of the Parivrājaka chief Hastin, the contemporary of Sarvanātha of Uchchakalpa. He is said to have governed Dabhālā (possibly

A.D.

Dahālā, *i.e.*, southern Baghelkhand), and the country included in the "eighteen forest kingdoms" (Khoh inscription of Sankshobha).—C. I. I., iii., 93–110; J. B. A., lviii. (i), 100.

484 G. E., 165. Inscription on a pillar at Eran, in Saugor District, 174, 18-(?), on coins, show one Budhagupta ruling in Mālwā. The actual connection of Budhagupta with the Gupta dynasty of Māgadha is unknown, but he was certainly of the same family. He was apparently defeated between the years 494 and 510 A.D. by the Huna adventurer Toramāna.—C. I. I., iii., 88-89; J. R. A. S., xxi., 134; *ib.* 1893, 86.

490 The rise of the Valabhi dynasty (490–770) took place about this time under Bhatārka of Maitraka race. The earlier kings were subject to the Hunas. After the destruction of the Huna rule, however, they rose to great power ruling from Valabhī, the present Walā (near Bhaunagar), and Anhilwāra Pātan; their dominion including much of Western Mālwā as far as Ratlām and Sailāna.—A. S. W. I., ii., 80; vi., 3; ix., 4; I. A., xv., 273; Ep. Ind., viii., 188 (Ratlām plates).

Toramāna the Huna penetrated to Gwalior, and finally into Mālwā, which he seized from the petty local Gupta and other chiefs, ruling there from 490–510. Three of his inscriptions are known; (1) at Eran in the Saugor District, dated in first year of his reign (C. I. I., iii., 159); (2) at Kewra, in the Salt Range near Jhelam (E. I., i., 238); and (3) at Gwalior, dated in the 15th year of his son Mihirakula (C. I. I., iii., 161). Coins are also known (J. A. B., xiii., 1195).—*See Early Hist.*, 273; I. A., xviii., 225; xxxiv. (1905), 73. Stein-*Rājātarangini*.

510. Mihirakula succeeds his father Toramāna. He overthrew the Gupta power in Western and Central India, and ruled till finally defeated at Mandasor about 530 A.D. by Yashodharman. The capital of his dominion was Sākala, in the Punjab. Coins bearing Mihirakula's name have been found at Shāhkot, in the Punjab.—J. A. B., 1894, *see* under 490.

528 G. E., 209. Copper-plate of the Parivrājaka Mahārājā Sanskhoba, son and successor of Hastin.—C. I. I., iii., 112.

533 V. Sam., 589. Inscription at Mandasor. Mihirakula's cruel and oppressive rule caused a revolt, and Yashodharman, apparently a prince ruling at Mandasor, of whom, however, nothing further is known, combined with Bālāditya of Māgadha to destroy the tyrant. A fight took place near Mandasor, where Mihirakula was defeated.—I. A., xv., 222, 245, 252; C. I. I., iii., 142; J. B. A., lviii. (i), 95.

550 A Sīlāditya of "Molapo" (Mālwā?) is mentioned by Hiuen Tsiang. But both the King's and the country's identity are in dispute.—Beal, *Records*, ii., 260; J. R. A. S., 1903, 553.

A.D.

585 Prabhākaravardhana of Thānesar rises to power by defeating the Hunas in the Panjāb, and also the Gurjaras. His mother was a Gupta.—*Early History*, 282; J. B. R. A. S., 1903, 545; C. I. I., iii.; E. I., i., 67; iv., 208.

600 Grahavarman, the Maukhari, who was either king or governor of Kanauj, married Rājyasrī, daughter of Prabhākaravardhana of Thānesar. One Devagupta appears to have been ruling Eastern Mālwā at this time. J. B. A., lviii. (i), chart p. 100. J. R. A. S., 1908, 765.

605 Grahavarman is killed by the Mālwā king, who imprisons Rājyasrī. To avenge his brother-in-law's death. Rājyavardhana of Thānesar, eldest son and successor of Prabhākaravardhana, goes on an expedition against the Mālwā king, whom he defeats. On his way home, however, he is attacked and killed by Sasānka of Central Bengal.—E. I., i., 70; J. R. A. S., 1905, 1.

606 Saka 528, *Kārtik badi* 1*st*. Oct. 22nd. The initial year of the Harsha era. This year commences from the succession of Harshvardhana. Harsha was the most famous ruler of his line. His first act was to rescue his sister Rājyasrī, who had been seized by Sasānka. He then proceeded to extend his dominions in all directions until his empire stretched from the basin of the Ganges (including Nepāl) and the Himālaya to the Narbadā, all the local chiefs being his feudatories. By incessant touring in his dominions, he continued to maintain his power throughout this vast tract.

He was a great patron of learning and of literary men, and the rise of the artificial court epic or *Kāvya* dates from his reign. The famous poet Bāna, the author of the *Sri-Harsha-charita*, of which Harsha is the hero, and of the *Kādambari*, was a resident at his court.—Macdonell, *Sanskrit Literature*, 318. *Sri-harsha-charita*, translated by Cowell and Thomas. *Kādambari*, translated by C. M. Ridding.

630 The Chinese pilgrim and traveller Hiuen Tsiang visits India (630–645). In his travels he visits Harsha's court at Kanauj, and also goes (641) to Jajhoti (Bundelkhand) where he visits Khajrāho.—Beale, *Buddhist records of the Western World* and *Life of Hiuen Tsiang*. Cunningham. *Ancient Geography*.

639 G. E. 320, 321. Ratlām plates of Dhruvasena II., Vallabhī of Gujarāt showing their possession of south-western Mālwā.—E. I., viii., 188; Arch. Survey Report, 1902–03, 232.

645 Hiuen Tsiang leaves India.

648 Death of Harshavardhana. His throne was usurped by his Minister Arjuna and the empire fell to pieces. The kings of Central India, hitherto subject to Harsha, now found themselves free to follow their own bent without restraint. This resulted in the formation of numerous

A.D.

principalities in constant feud with one another, and consequently from this date till the Muhammadan conquest no native ruler held paramount power in Northern India. The petty states thus left to their own devices, without a superior controlling power, by their incessant internal wars, opened the way to Muhammadan conquest.

690 The poet Bhavabhūti of Ujjain flourished at this time. The scene of his play *Mālatī-Mādhava* is laid in Ujjain.—Macdonell. *Sanskrit Literature*, 362. *Mālatī Mādhava*. Edited by Bhandārkar. *Preface*.

724 H. 106. Junaid-ibn-Abdur-Rahman al Marri attacks Ujjain. E. M. H., i., 441.

746 V. Sam. 802. Vana-rāja founds the Chāvada dynasty of Anhilwāra.—Forbes, *Rās Māla*. I. A., vi., 182. Bombay Gazetteer, *Gujarāt*.

800 Rise of the Paramaras of Mālwā.

The great Gūrjara clan had since the death of Harsha acquired possession of Gujarāt, Mālwā and Bundelkhand. Of this clan two sections predominated, the Paramāras and Parihārs, the former holding Mālwā and the latter Bundelkhand, apparently under a Gurjara overlord. Later on these two sections threw off their suzerainty and became independent.

The Paramāra chief of that day was named Upendra-rājā or Krishna-rāja. His family seems to have originally lived at Abu. Upendra was succeeded, so far as our knowledge goes, by 19 other chiefs in the direct line. Of the first five, Upendra-rājā, Vaira-sinha I., Siyaka I., Vākpati I., and Vairasinha II., only the names are known. The most famous of the line were Vākpati-rājā (Munja) and the famous scholar-king Bhoja I., the Augustus of India.—E. I., i., 222; ii., 180. I. A., xix., 345. *See* Appendix to *Dhar State Gazetteer* and Dynastic list, page 82.

831 About this time the Chandellas, who had been rising in power in Bundelkhand since the death of Harshvardhana, contrived under the leadership of Nānika to overthrow the Parihār dynasty and seize Bundelkhand, then known as Jajaka-bhukti, or the province of Jejaka, subsequently corrupted to Jajhoti. Of this line 23 kings are known whose rule extended up to 1288. The best known are Dhanga (955 to 999), Ganda (999 to 1025), Kirtivarman (1098 to 1100), and Parmārdideva or Parmāl (1167 to 1213). After the defeat of Parmārdideva in 1182 by Prithvi-rāja, the Chauhān king of Delhi, they became petty local chiefs.—*Early History*, 312. J. A. B., l. (i) 1. I. A., xxxvii, 141.

862 V. Sam. 932, 933. Gwalior inscription of Bhojadeva of Kanauj, in the Chatarbhūj rock-cut temple.—E. I., i., 154. *See also* E. I., i., 184. I. A., xvii., 23; xix., 28; xx., 188. C. A. S. R., x., 101.

900 Harshadeva Chandella succeeds Rāhila. Undated record at Khajrāho.—E. I., i., 121, 171. C. A. S. R., ii., 451.

A.D.

903 V. Sam. 960. Terahi (Gwalior) inscription.—I. A., xvii., 201.

925 Yasovarman (Lākshvarman) Chandella, son and successor of Harshadeva; he is represented as overcoming many tribes, among whom were the Mālavas, Chedis of Bhagelkhand, and the Gurjaras. From the Chedi kings he captured the fort of Kālanjar, and thus consolidated the Chandella power.—E. I., i., 122 ff. C. A. S. R., ii., 451. I. A., xviii., 237.

Keyuravarsha-Yuvarājadeva I., Kalachuri of Chedi succeeds his brother Bālaharsha.—C. A. S. R., ix., 100. E. I., ii., 304.

941 Founding of the Solanki or Chaulukya (Chālukya) dynasty of Anhilwāra (Gujarāt) by Mulrāja I., who drove out the Chāvadas. The dynasty numbered 13 kings, and ruled till about 1230.—Bombay Gazetteer, *Gujarat*. Forbes, *Rās Māla*.

Sīyaka II., *alias* Harsha, Paramāra of Mālava, succeeds Vairasinha II. He married Vadajā. He conquered the Rāshtrakūta king Khottiga and others.—E. I., i., 225.

955 V. Sam. 1011. Monday, 2nd April. Khajrāho inscription of Dhanga, Chandella. His dominion extended from the Jamna to the Narbadā and from Kālanjar to Gwalior. Some of the famous temples at Khajrāho are his work. He joined Rāja Jaipāl of Lahore in 978 against Sabuktagīn, taking part in the defeat at Laghmān.—E. I., i., 135, 137, 218; I. A., xvi., 201; B. F., i., 18.

956 V. Sam. 1013. Inscription from Suhāniya in Gwalior of one Mahendra-chandra, son of Mādhava. It is not known if he was a rājā of Gwalior or not. J. B. A., xxxi., 399.

B.—The Muhammadan Period, 970 to 1707 A.D.

I.—THE PATHĀN KINGS, 970 TO 1527 A.D.

[NOTE.—*The Chiefs in Central India were not actually brought into contact with the Muhammadans till about* 980, *but their advance into India dates some time before this.*]

A.D.

970 Birth of Mahmūd of Ghaznī, son of Sabuk-tagīn. R. T., 44, 76. B. F., (i), 33. E. M. H., ii, 269.

972 V. Sam. 1029. Dhanapāla, a poet protégé of the Mālwa Paramāras, writes the *Pāiyalachchhī*, and other works. —I. A., ii., 166; iv., 59. A. C. 267.

973 Chedi Sam. 724. Chandrehi (Rewah) inscription of the ascetic Prasāntasiva. I.A., xx., 95.

974 V. Sam. 1031, 1036. Ujjain copper plates. Vākpati II. (Munja).—*See under* 800. I. A., vi., 51; xiv., 160.

A.D.

He is credited with defeating the Chedi ruler Yuvarāja. He is also credited with defeating Tailapa II., the Western Chālukya (973–997), but was ultimately conquered and put to death by this king.—Ep. In., vi., 222, 251; ii, 304. Bom. Gaz., i., 424.

977 V. Sam. 1034. Inscription from Suhāniya (Gwalior) of Vajradāman of the Kachchha-paghāta (Kachhwāha) family who is said in the Sāsbāhu record to have captured Gwalior from a ruler of Kanauj.—J. A. B., xxxi., 393, 401, 411. I. A., xv., 35.

979 V. Sam. 1036. Ujjain copper plate of Mūnja-Vākpati II., Paramāra of Mālwā.—I. A., xiv., 159.

H., 369. Jaipāl of Lahore marches on Ghaznī, but retires.—R. T., 74, n, 2.

980 Parimāla or Padmagupta, who was poet laureate under the Paramāra kings Vākpati (A.D. 974–995) and Sindhurāja (A.D. 995–1010), writes the *Navasāhasānka-charita*, a poem in honour of Sindhurājā. To Munja's time belong also the poets Dhananjaya, author of the *Dasharupa*, and his brother Dhanika, author of the *Dasharupavaloka*, also Halāyudha, author of the *Pingalachhandashtīkā*.—Macdonell, *Sanskrit Literature*, 331, 434. E. I., i., 227. I. A., xxxvi., 162. Appendix to *Dhār State Gazetteer*.

988 H. 378. Sabuktagīn again encounters Jaipāl and defeats him at Laghmān. Jaipal was allied with all the great Hindu chiefs, including the "Rājā of Kālanjar," viz., Dhanga Chandella.—R. T., 74.

997 Sindhurāja (*Navasāhasānka*) Paramāra of Mālwā, brother and successor of Vākpati II. He fought with Chamunda-rājā, the Chaulukya of Anhilwāra (996–1009).—E. I., i., 228 ff.; 294. I. A., vi., 184; xxxvi, 162. Forbes. *Rās Mālā*. *See under* 800.

998 V. Sam. 1055. Copper plate grant of Dhanga Chandella. I. A., xvi., 201.

Another inscription of V. Sam., 1059 at Khajrāho was erected after his death.—Ep. Ind., i., 140.

999 Ganda or Nanda Chandella, son and successor of Dhanga. He joined the Hindu confederacy raised by Anandpāl, Rājā of Lahore, which tried in vain to stem the advance of Mahmūd of Ghaznī in 1009.—C. A. S. R., ii., 451; xxi., 84. Ep. Ind., i., 219.

1001 H. 391. Mahmūd of Ghaznī in *Shāwal* (August to September) makes his first expedition to India, and defeats Jaipāl of Lahore near Peshawar on 8th Muharram, 392 H. (27th November).

Ferishta's date of H. 390 seems wrong.—R. T., 81. E. M. H., ii., 26, 435. B. F., i., 37, ff.

V. Sam. 1058, 1205. Record of Grahapati family at Khajrāho.—E. I., i., 148.

A.D.

1006 H. 396. Mahmūd's second expedition to India. He reaches Multān.—E. M. H., iv., 172. R. T., 84, 85.

1009 H. 399. Mahmūd's fifth expedition takes place. He again defeats the Lahore king, Anandpāl, successor of Jaipāl, and a Hindu confederacy at Batindah.—E. M. H., ii., 443. R. T., 76, note.

V. Sam. 1066. Vallabharāja succeeds to the Gujarāt kingdom, but dies soon after, and is followed by Durlabha. Vallabha invaded Mālwā.—I. A., vi., 184, 213. E. I., i., 294.

1010 Bhoja or Bhojadeva Paramāra of Dhār, son and successor of Sindhurājā. One of the most famous rulers of the 11th century, celebrated throughout India for his learning and patronage of literary men. He fought the Chālukya king Jayasimha III., between A.D. 1011 and 1019, and also his successor Somesvara II. (A.D. 1042–1068), who according to Bilhana's *Vikramānka-deva-charita*, took Dhār by storm, and forced Bhoja to flee. Bhoja conquered the Chaulukya Bhīma I. (A.D. 1021–1063), and took Anhilwāra (Merutunga-*Prabandhachintāmani*). Al-Biruni mentions his reigning in A.D. 1030, while his work, the *Rājmrigānkakarana*, is dated S. 964 (A.D. 1042). The exact date of his death is not yet known, but about 1053 he was driven from his kingdom by a confederacy of the kings of Gujarāt and Chedi, and the Paramāra power declined from this time. *See under* 800.

1013 Between 1013 and 1021, Mahmūd of Ghazni made five more expeditions into India, the 8th (1013), 9th (1014), 10th (1015), 11th (1018), and 12th (1021).—E. M. H., ii., 37, 450, 452, 455, 456, 463. R. T., 85. B. F., i., 63.

1021 Mahmūd makes his 12th advance into India, to rescue his feudatory, the King of Kanauj, who had been attacked by the Chandella king, Ganda.—E. M. H., ii., 463.

V. Sam. 1078. Ujjain grant of Bhojadeva of Dhār.—I. A., vi., 53.

1022 V. Sam. 1078. Bhīmadeva I. Chaulukya succeeds Durlabharāja. He joined Karna Chedi in attacking Dhār, and Bhoja was forced to fly.—*See Kīrtikaumudi.* I. A., vi., 185, 213. E. I., i., 232, 294; *also under* 800.

1023 H. 413, 414. Mahmūd again invades India and attacks Gwalior, but is bought off, and then proceeds to Kālanjar, where he forces Ganda the Chandella to come to terms. E. M. H., ii., 434 ff., especially 467. B. F., i., 66, 67. R. T., 86.

1025 Vidhyādhara Chandella succeeded his father, Ganda.—E. I., i., 219; ii., 235.

1026 H. 416. 4th January. Mahmūd takes Somnāth.—E. M. H., i., 98; iv., 180. B. G. 28. I. A., vi., 185. R. T., 82.

A.D.

1030 H. 421. *Rabi II.* 23. Thursday, 30th April. Mahmūd dies, and Muhammad succeeds, but is ousted by Masūd.—E.M.H. iv., 192.

1037 Vijayapāla Chandella succeeds Vidhyādhara.—E. I., i., 219.

1038 Chedi Sam., 789; Piāwan (Rewah) inscription of Gangeyadeva Kalachuri. Albiruni mentions that Gangeyadeva was ruler of Dāhālā. He reigned probably till about A.D. 1040.—C. A. S. R., xxi., 113. E. I., ii., 304.

1040 Dhār was captured by the western Chālukya king Somesvara II., and Bhoja was forced to flee.—Bombay Gazetteer, i., 438. *See under* 800.

1042 The Udayapura inscriptions state that Udayāditya Paramārā of Mālwā overthrew Gangeyadeva's successor Karna Chedi (1042–1122) and delivered the earth, "which was troubled by kings and taken possession of by Karna." Karna was also defeated by the Chandella general, Gopāla, under King Kirtivarman, as is recorded in inscriptions and in the *Prabodhachandrodaya.*—*Vikramancharita,* 18, 95. I. A., xvii., 215. E. I., ii., 297. C. A. S. R., ix., 82.

1050 V. S. 1107. Nanyaura plate. Devavarman Chandella succeeds Vijayāpala, his father.—I. A., xvi., 204. E. I., i., 219. C. A. S. R., xxi., 81.

1053 Probable date of the final defeat of Bhoja by the combined forces of Gujarāt and Chedi under Bhīma Deva I. and Karna.—Kāthvate, *Kīrtikaumudi,* Introduction. E. I., i., 232, 290. I. A., vi., 185.

1055 V. Sam. 1112. Mandhāta plate. Jayasinha Paramāra succeeds Bhoja in Mālwā.—E. I., iii., 46.

1059 V. Sam. 1116 and S. 981 Inscription of Udayāditya Paramāra, at Udayapura.—J. A. O. S., vii. 24. J. A. B., ix., 545.

1080 V. Sam. 1137. The Udayapura temple inscription Udayāditya Paramāra of Mālwā, successor of Jayasinha. In the Nāgpur prasasti he is said to have freed the land from the dominion of Karna of Chedi.—I. A., xx., 83. E. I., i., 223; ii., 181; iii., 47, 48. C. A. S. R., ix., 109.

1085 Lakshmadeva Paramāra of Mālwā, son and successor of Udayāditya, according to the Nāgpur prasasti.—E. I., ii., 182.

1088 V. Sam. 1145. Dubkund (Gwalior) inscription. Vikramāsinha Kachchhapaghāta, son and successor of Vijayapāla.—E. I., ii., 232 ff.

1090 The poet Krishna-misra flourished at the Court of the Chandella Kīrtivarman. His play, the *Prabodhachandrodaya,* is of unusual merit.—Macdonell, *Sanskrit Literature,* 366. *Prabodhachandrodaya,* translated by J. Taylor. (1812.) E. I., i., 220.

A.D.

1093 V. Sam. 1150. Sâsbahu temple inscription (Gwalior) of Mahipāla Bhuvanaikamalla, son of Suryapāla of the Kachchhapaghāta or Kachchhapāri race, the successor of Padmapāla.—I. A., xv., 33 ff. C. A. S. R., ii., 357. T. P. K. 63. J. B. A., xxxi., 400.

V. Sam. 1150. Jayasimha-Siddhrâja, Chaulukya succeeded his father, Karna I., till 1143. He conquered Yasovarman of Mālwā, "the lord of Avanti." I. A., vi., 186; x., 158. E. I., i., 295.

1097 V. Sam. 1154. Grant of Madanapāladeva, son of the Gaharwār Chandradeva, of Kanauj. Chandradeva, is said to have quelled the disturbances which arose on the death of the Paramāra King, Bhoja.—J.A.B., xxvii., 220. I. A., xviii., 9.

1098 V. Sam. 1154. Sunday, 7th March. Deogarh inscription. Kīrtivarman Chandella, brother and successor of Devavarman. Karna Chedi was defeated by Kīrtivarman's general, Gopāla. — *Prabodhachandrodaya*, translated by J. Taylor. (1812.) C. A. S. R., x., 102, 103, pl. xxxiii., 3; xxi., 81. I. A., xi., 311; xviii, 237. E. I., i., 219 ff.

1100 Sallakshanavarmadeva Chandella succeeds his father, Kīrtivarman. He is said to have defeated the Chedis and Mālavas.—E. I., i., 196, 326.

1104 V. Sam. 1161–64. Nāgpur and Madhukargarh inscription of Naravarman Paramāra of Mālwā, brother and successor of Lakshmadeva, according to the Nāgpur inscription. Other inscriptions make him immediate successor of Udayāditya. He reigned till 1133.—E. I., ii., 180. J. R. A. S., i., 207, 226. Colebrooke *Essays*, ii., 229.

V. Sam. 1161. Inscription at Gwalior recording erection of a temple by Madhusudana, son of Bhuvanapāla, the successor of Mahīpāla.—C. A. S. R., ii., 364. J. B. A., xxxi., 403, 418. I. A., xv., 201.

1117. V. Sam. 1173. Khajrāho inscription of Jayavarman Chandella, son and successor of Sallakshanavarman.—E. I., 139.

1120 V. Sam. 1177. Narwar copper-plate grant. Virasinhadeva Kachchhapaghāta.—J. A. O. S., vi., 542. E. I., ii., 234. C. A. S. R., ii., 312.

1129 V. Sam. 1186–1222, on inscriptions. Madanavarmadeva Chandella, son and successor of Prithvīvarman. He defeated the kings of Chedi and Mālwā.—(*Mau inscription.*) C. A. S. R., xxi. E. I., i., 95.

1133 V. Sam. 1190. Augāsī copper-plate of the Chandella Madanavarmadava.—I. A., xvi., 207.

Yasovarmadeva Paramāra of Mālwā succeeds his father Naravarman; copper-plates of V. Sam. 1191 and 1192—Colebrooke's *Essays*, ii., 299 ff. I. A., xix., 348, 351.

V. Sam 1190. Ingnoda (Dewās) inscription of Vijayapāladeva Paramāra.—I. A., vi., 55.

A.D.

1136 V. Sam. 1192. Ujjain plates of Yasovarman Paramāra. —I. A., xix., 349.

1138 Jayavarman Paramāra of Mālwā succeeds his father, Yashovarman. He appears to have been dethroned by his brother, Ajayavarman. Up to Yashovarman, the later records of the Paramāras agree as to the succession. The dynasty under Yashovarman's successors seems to have split into two branches: Ajayavarman, Vindhayavarman, Subhatavarman, and Arjunvarman represented the main line, while Lakshmivarman, Harischandra, and Udayavarman represented a separate line, whose right to rule rested on the claims of Jayavarman.—I. A., xix., 348, 349. *See under* 800.

1143 V. Sam. 1199. Kumārapala Chaulukya of Anhilwāra succeeds his uncle Jayasinha-Siddharāja. He conquers Mālwā—Forbes, *Rās Māla* I. A., vi., 213. E. I., 293; ii., 421. *Rājasthan*, i., 707.

1144 V. Sam. 1200. 16th July. Copper plate from Ujjain, of Lakshmivarmadeva Paramāra of Mālwā, son of Yashovarman.—*See* 1138. I. A. xix., 348, 351.

1149 V. Sam. 1205. Khajrāho inscription of the Grahapati family.—E. I., i. 153.

1152 V. Sam. 1208. The Vadnagar inscription of Kumārapāla Chaulukya.—Ep. Ind., i., 296.

1155 Chedi Sam. 907. Beraghāt inscription of Alhanadevī.—Ep. Ind., ii., 7.

V. Sam. 1211. Mahoba image inscription of Madanavarman Chandella.—C. A. S. R., xxi., 73.

1158 V. Sam. 1215. Khajrāho inscription of Madanavarman Chandella.—E. I., i. 153.

Chedi Sam. 909. Wednesday, 2nd July. Lāl-Pahār. or Bharhūt inscription of Narasinhadeva Kalachuri of Chedi.—I. A., xviii., 211.

1159 Alhāghāt (Rewah) inscription of Narasinhadeva Kalachuri.—I. A., xviii., 213.

1160 Vindhyavarman Paramāra of Mālwā, son and successor of Ajayavarman.—J. B. A., xxx., 204.

1163 V. Sam. 1220 (?) Inscription at Udayapura (Gwalior) of Kumārapāla Chaulukya, showing he then possessed this tract, which had fallen to Gujarāt.—I. A., xviii., 341.

1166 V. Sam. 1222. Inscription on a pillar by Kumārapāla's general, at Udayapura in Gwalior.—I. A., xviii., 344.

1167 V. Sam. 1223. Semra inscription of Paramārdideva Chandella, son and successor Madana of varman, confirming an earlier grant of that ruler, of V. Sam. 1219.—E. I., iv., 153. For the numerous inscriptions of this king *see* C. A. S. R., ii., 444, 448; x., 96; xxi., 37, 49, 68, 71, 74, 81. I.A., xxv, 205

A.D.

1168 V. Sam. 1224. Mahoba inscription of Parmārdideva Chandella.—I. A., xix., 36. C. A. S. R., xxi., 74.

1171 V. Sam. 1227. Ichchhāwar plates of Paramārdideva Chandella.—I. A., xxv., 205. J. A. B., lxix. (i.), 156.

1173 V. Sam. 1229. Grant of Ajayapāla Chaulakya at Udayapura (Gwalior), showing that the Gujarāt rulers still held this region.—I. A., xviii., 347.

1175 Chedi Sam. 926; Rewah copper-plate of the Maharānaka Kīrtivarman of Kakkaredī, son and successor of Vatsarājā, and feudatory of Jayasinhadeva Kalachuri of Chedi, the brother and successor of Narasimhadeva. —I. A., xvii., 224.

1178 Muīz-ud-Dīn (Shihab-ud-dīn) attacks Bhīmadeva of Gūjarāt but is defeated. This marks the entry of Muhammadans into Western India.—Forbes. *Rās Māla*, i., 65. R. T., 451. T. P. K., 11. E. M. H., ii., 294. B. G., 34.

V. Sam. 1235, 1236. Pipliānagar grant of Harischandra Paramāra of Mālwā successor of Lakshmivarman.—J. B. A., vii., 736.

1182 V. Sam. 1239. Prithvirājā the Chauhān conquers the Chandella king Paramārdideva (Parmāl) of Jejakabhukti (Bundelkhand) according to inscriptions from Madanpur. The *Prithvirāj Rāso* of Chand puts the event in V. Sam. 1241 or 1184 A.D.—A. S. N. I., ii., 124. *Early Hist.*, 310. C. A. S. R., x., 98; xxi., 173.

1187 V. Sam. 1234. Ajaigarh fort gate inscription.—C. A. S. R., xxi., 50.

1190 The poet Chand, author of the well-known *Prithvirāj Rāso* flourished at this time apparently. He was contemporary with Prithvirāja the Chauhān.—I. A., i., 269.

1191 Prithvirāja (Pithora Rai) Chauhān of Ajmir advances with other Hindu princes and defeats Muiz-ud-dīn, at Tarain, near Thānesar. The latter who was wounded retired to Lahore.—E. M. H., ii., 295. R.T., 457 and notes.

1192 Muiz-ud-dīn returns to Hindustān, again encounters Prithvirājā and his allies near Thānesar, and totally defeats them, thus becoming master of the country. Prithvirājā was captured and put to death, his son being appointed Governor of Ajmir.—R. T., 457, 464, 466, *note*, 469, 516. E. M. H., ii., 216. T. P. K., 33.

1193 H. 589. Kutb-ud-dīn captures Delhi. Muiz-ud-dīn makes it the capital of the Muhammadan power in Hindustān.—R. T., 469. J. B. A., xliv. (i), 275; xlv. (i), 325 ff. B. M. C., *Sultāns of Delhi*, xii., xxxiii. T. P. K., 23.

Kutb-ud-dīn takes Kālanjar and Mahoba.—R. T., 523 ff. E. M. H., ii., 231.

1194 Kutb-ud-dīn takes Kanauj.—R. T., 470.

A.D.

1195 V. Sam. 1258. Sunday, 19th September. Bagrāri or Batesvar stone inscription of the Chandella Paramārdideva.—E. I., i., 207.

V. Sam. 1253. Friday, 27th October. Rewah copper plate of Vijayasinhadeva Kalachuri of Chedi, son and successor of Jayasinhadeva and of his feudatory Salakshanavarmadeva Mahārānaka of Kakaredī, son of Vatsarāja, brother and successor of Kīrtivarman.—I. A., xvii., 227.

Kutb-ud-dīn defeats Bhīmadeva Chaulukya's general and sacks Anhilwāra.—R. T., 516, *note*. E. I., i., 22.

1196 H. 592. Muiz-ud-dīn proceeded to Gwalior and left Bahau-ud-dīn Tughril to reduce it. After a year's siege its Parihār chief surrendered to Kutb-ud-dīn. Shams-ud-dīn Altamsh was appointed governor by Kutb-ud-dīn.—R. T., 470 and *note*, 3, 517, *note*, 518, 520, 546, 604. E. M. H., ii., 227, 304, 322.

1200 V. Sam. 1256. Sunday, 30th April. Copper plate from Bhopāl. Udayavarmadeva Paramāra of Mālwā, son of Harischandra and successor of Lakshmīvarmadeva.—I. A., xvi., 252.

1201 V. Sam. 1258. Kālanjar record of Paramārdideva Chandella.—J. B. A., xvii., 313; I. A., xix., 354.

1202 Parmārdideva Chandella defeated at Kālanjar by Kutb-ud-dīn.—E. M. H., ii., 231.

1206 H. 602. Muiz-ud-dīn is assassinated and Kutb-ud-dīn establishes himself in Hindustān, being crowned at Lahore, 18*th Zil q'adah* (26th June).—R. T., 398, 484, 493, 522, note.

1210 H. 607. Kutb-ud-dīn Aibak dies at Lahore, and Altamsh seizes the throne. R. T. 528–9.

1211 V. Sam. 1267, 1270 and 1272. Thursday, 24th February. On copper plates from Pīplianagar in Bhopāl. Arju navarmadeva Paramāra of Mālwā, son and successor of Subhatavarman, whose predecessors were his father, Vindhyavarman, and grandfather, Ajayavarman, the latter being probably a son of Yasovarman and brother of Jayarvarman, whom he deposed. Arjunavarman was the author of the *Rasikasanjīvinī*, a commentary on the *Amarusataka*.—*See* A.D. 1138. J. B. A. v., 377. J. A. O. S. vii., 25, 32. I. A. xix., 24. Z. D. M. G. xlvii., 92.

1213 V. Sam. 1269 and 1298. Trailokyavarmadeva Chandolla, son and successor of Paramārdideva. Ajaigarh inscription.—C. A. S. R., xxi., 50, 147.

V. Sam. 1270. Arjunavarman Paramāra's grant issued from Brighukachchha (Broach).—J. A. O. S., vii., 32.

1215 V. Sam. 1272. Arjunavarman Paramāra's grant issued from Amareshwar on the Narbadā.—J. A. O. S., vii., 25.

1218 V. Sam. 1275. Saturday, 24th November, Harsauda inscription, Devapāladeva ruling at Dhār. Two inscriptions at Udayapura in Gwalior give him the date

A.D.

V. Sam. 1286 and 128(9)? The evidence of the Harsauda inscription establishes his connection with the Paramāra rulers, Lakshmivarman, Harischandra and Udayavarmadeva.—I. A. xix., 24; xx. 310.

1219 Rise of the Vaghela or Baghelas of Anhilwāra, the ancestors of the present Rewah house.—I. A. vi., 190, 213. *Kīrtikaumudi*, edited by Kāthvate, xiv., xv.; Bombay Gazetteer, *Gujarat*. Forbes, *Rās Māla*.

1224 V. Sam. 1280–90 on coins, Malayavarmadeva of Narwar then reigning.—T. P. K., 67, 74. J. B. A., xxxiv., 127.

1229 V. Sam. 1286. Inscription of Devapāladeva Paramāra at Udayapura in Gwalior.—I. A., xx., 83.

1231 H. 629. Altamsh beseiges Gwalior, which, after being taken by Kutb-ud-dīn Aibak, had been lost to the Musalmāns during the disturbances that arose on the latter's death.—R. T., 619. E. M. H., ii., 327.

1232 H. 639, 12th December (26th Safar). Altamsh takes the fort of Gwalior after 11 months' siege.—R. T., 620. E. M. H., ii., 327.

V. Sam. 128 (9)? Devapāla Paramāra's inscription.—(*See* 1218.)

1234 H. 631. Nusrat-ud-dīn Tāyasi invades Kālanjar from Gwalior. The Rājā retreating discomfited, he plundered the towns and took vast booty. On his return, Chāhadadeva, Rājā of Narwar, intercepts him, but Nusrat-ud-dīn defeats him and returns to Gwalior. In the same year he is appointed to the superintendency of the Gwalior territory.—R. T., 732. T. P. K., 67.

1235 H. 632. Altamsh takes Bhīlsa and Ujjain.—R. T., 621. E. M. H., ii., 327.

1236 On his return, Altamsh is seized with illness and dies (April).—E. M. H., ii., 318.

1239 V. Sam. 1297. Rewah copper plate of the Mahārānaka Kumārapāla of Kakaredī, son of Harirājā and feudatory of the Chandella Trailokyavarman.—I. A., xvii., 230.

1241 V. Sam. 1298. Rewah copper plate of Mahārānka Harirājā of Kakaredi, son of Salakhshanavarman and father of Kumārapāla, whose copper plate, however, issued in V. Sam. 1297. He was a feudatory of Trailokyavarman.—(*See* A.D. 1213.) I. A., xvii., 234.

1243 V. Sam. 1300. Visaladeva Vaghela (Baghela) usurps the throne of Anhilwāra.—E. I., i. 20. I. A., vi. 212. Bom. Gaz., *Gujarat*. Forbes, *Rās-Māla*.

1247 V. Sam. 1303–11 on coins. Chāhādadeva of Narwar, successor of Malayavarmadeva.—T. P. K., 75. J. B. A., xxxiv., 127. J. B. A., 1905, 262.

1248 H. 645. Ulugh Khān defeats "Dalakī-wa-Malakī," apparently a Bundelkhand chief.—E. M. H., ii., 348–366. R. T., 682. B. F., i., 237.

A.D.

1251 H. 649, 25*th Shabān* (12 Nov.). Ulugh Khān (Balban) proceeds against Gwalior, Chanderi, and Narwar, and Mālwā for Nāsir-ud-dīn of Delhi. Defeats Chāhādadeva and takes Narwar.—R. T., 690, 842. T. P. K., 67, 125. E. M. H., ii., 351, 368.

1255 V. Sam. 1311–1330. Dates found on coins and inscriptions. Asāladeva of Narwar, son of Naravarman, successor of Chahādeva.—J. B. A., xxxiv., 127.

1256 V. Sam. 1312. Inscriptions at Rāhatgarh of the Paramāra Jayasinhadeva, ruling at Dhār.* The Udayapura record of V. S. 1311 may also refer to him.—I. A., xx., 84.

1261 V. S. 1317 and 1318. Ajaigarh and Jhānsi records of Virāvarman Chandella, son of Trailokyavarman (till 1337).—E. I., i., 325. C. A. S. R., xxi., 38, 51, 52, 74. I. A., xix., 179.

1266 H. 664. Ulugh Khān succeeds as Ghiās-ud-dīn Balban. He dies in 1387.—T. P. K., 131. E. M. H., i., 341; iii., 97. B. F., i., 246.

1268 V. Sam. 1325, 1337, and 1342. Ajaigarh inscriptions of Viravarman Chandella.—C. A. S. R., xxi., 51, 52, 174.

1269 V. Sam. 1326. Pathārī inscription of Jayasinhadeva of Dhār.

1289 V. Sam. 1345–72. Bhojavarman Chandella, son and successor of Viravarman. Inscriptions at Ajaigarh.—J. B. A., vi., 882. C. A. S. R., xxi., 52. Ep. Ind., i., 330.

1291 H. 690. Firuz Shāh sacks Ujjain and destroys many temples in Mālwā.—E. M. H., iii., 146, 540. T. P. K., 144. B. F., i., 301.

1292 V. Sam. 1348 and 1355 (26 Sept. 1298, A.D.). Sarwāya and Narwar Inscp. of Ganapati of Narwar, son and successor of Gopāla.—I. A., xxii., 81.

1293 H. 692. Firuz Shāh invades and plunders Mālwā a second time, and his nephew Alā-ud-dīn takes Bhīlsa and reduces eastern Mālwā.—E. M. H., iii., 148.

1296 H. 695. Firuz Shāh is assassinated by Alā-ud-din, who succeeds.—T. P. K., 144, 154. E. M. H., iii., 69, 150. B. F., i., 311.

1298 H. 698 (or 696 and 697). Ulugh Khān and Nasrat Khān invade Gujarāt, sack Somnāth, and drive out the Bāghelas or Vāghelas, who found a new dynasty in Rewah.—E. M. H., iii., 43, 74, 163, 551. B. F., i., 327. B. G., 37. *Rewah State Gazetteer.*

1300 The Barwānī State was founded about this time.

1301 H. 700. Ujjain taken by Ala-ud-dīn.—E. M. H., iii., 75, 175.

1305 H. 705. Mālwā is invaded by Ain-ul-Mulk, and Rai Malak Deo and his Pradhān Koka, are defeated, and Ujjain, Chanderi, Māndu, and Dhār are taken. —E. M. H., iii., 76. B. F., i., 361.

---

* Called Jaitugideva elsewhere, *see* B. R., 1883–4, 105, 392.

A.D.

1310 V. Sam. 1366. Udayapura (in Gwalior) temple inscription of Mahārāja Jayasinhadeva, probably the ruler of Dhār.—I. A., xx., 84.

1316 H. 715. Jan. 5. Alā-ud-dīn dies.—T. P. K., 176, 177. E. M. H., iii., 208.

1321 H. 720. Ghiās-ud-dīn Tughlak ascends the throne.—E. M. H., i., 344; iii, 228.

1325 H. 725. Death of Ghiyās-ud-dīn Tughlak. Muḥammad Tughlak succeeds.—T. P. K., 189. E. M. H., iii., 235. B. F., i., 406.

1340 V. Sam. 1397. Kevati Kund (Bijāwar) records.—C. A. S. R., xxi., 143.

1343 H. 744. Famine in Mālwā.—E. M. H., iii., 244.

1344 H. 745. Azīz Himār sent to Mālwā. His tyrannous rule causes a revolt.—E. M. H., iii., 251. B. G., 43.

1348 V. Sam. 1404. Mārpha (Rewah) record of Sidhitunga; and Rāmpura (Rewah) inscription of Virarājadeva.—C. A. S. R., xxi, 19, 34.

1350 H. 751. Alā-ud-dīn Hasan Bāhmani marches on Māndu but the Governor buys him off.—I. A., xxviii., 152.

1351 H. 752. Firuz Shāh III. succeeds.—E. M. H., i., 225; iii., 263.

The Nāgod State was founded about this time.

1355 V. Sam. 1412. Inscriptions from Kāritālai (Nāgod) of one Viravarman of Uchahadanagar (Unchahra).—C. A. S. R., ix., plate ii., 3.

1387 H. 789. Dilāwar Khān made Governor of Mālwā.

1388 H. 790. Firuz Shāh dies, and Tughlak Shāh II. succeeds.—E. M. H., iv., 18. B. F., i., 461.

1397 H. 799. Muzaffar Shāh of Gujarāt attacks the "Rāja of Māndu" (Mandal-garh), and beseiges his fort.—B. G., 77.

1398 H. 800. Tīmūr sacks Delhi (26th Dec.).—E. M. H., iii., 433. B. F., i., 490.

Maḥmūd Shāh driven from Delhi seeks aid, first from Muzaffar of Gujarāt, and then from Dilāwar Khān of Mālwā.—B. G., 79.

1401 H. 804. Mahmūd Shāh returns to Delhi.—E. M. H., iv., 38.

Dilāwar Khān, Governor of Mālwā, assumes independence and founds the Ghori dynasty of Mālwā, ruling till H. 808 (A.D. 1405).—B. M. C. *Muh. States* 114 Intro.; Nu. Ch., 1904, 361. B. F., iv., 169.

1402 H. 805. December. Ikbal Khān marches on Gwalior, which had been wrested from the Muhammadans by one Nahar Singh, during the confusion of Timur's invasion. Nahar Singh's son and successor repulses Ikbal.—E. M. H., iv., 39.

1404 H. 807. Ikbal besieges Etāwah, where the "Rājā of Gwalior" and others are entrenched.—E. M. H., iv., 39. B. F., i., 501.

A.D.

1405 H. 808. Hoshang Shāh Ghori succeeds Dilāwar Khān as Sultān of Mālwā, till 838 (1434).—B. M. C., *Muhamm. States*, Intro. 114. Num. Chron., 1904. 62 ff. B. F., iv., 171.

1407 H. 810. Muzaffar Shāh of Gujarāt defeats Hoshang Shāh of Mālwā. In this year Hoshang commences the fortifications of Māndu.—E. M. H., iv., 41. B. F., i., 502.

Muzaffar now proceeds to conquer Mālwā, and Hoshang Shāh, who is besieged in Dhār, is taken prisoner. Nasrat Khān, brother of Muzaffar, becomes Governor of Mālwā.—B. G. 84.

1410 V. Sam. 1467. Inscription from Suhāniya (Gwalior) of Virangadeva (Bilangadeva) Tonwāra of Gwalior. —J. B. A., xxxi., 404, 422. C. A. S. R., ii., 401.

1413 H. 816. Hoshang Shāh of Mālwā, who had been set free, advances on Gujarāt, but retreats without fighting. —B. G., 95.

1416 H. 819. Malik-us-Shark is sent against Gwalior, which he plunders.—E. M. H., iv., 48.

Ahmad Shāh I. of Gujarāt, attacks Hoshang Shāh of Mālwa, who flees.—B. G., 99, note, 100. E. M. H., iv., 49.

1418 H. 821. Hoshang Shāh and Ahmad I. of Gujarāt fight at Kaliādeh, near Ujjain.—B. F., iv., 176. B. G., 102.

1419 H. 822. Ahmad I. of Gujarāt marches on Māndu, but at Dhār Hoshang comes to terms.—B. G., 104.

1421 H. 824. Khizr Khān invests Gwalior. He dies the same year, and is succeeded by Mubārak Shah II.—E. M. H., iv., 53.

1422 H. 825. *Rabi. I.* (March). Ahmad I. of Gujarāt captures Maheshwar (Indore State), and also invests Māndu (Ap. 5th), but retires to Ujjain after a seven weeks' siege. After the rains Ahmad again advances on Māndu, but Hoshang Shāh defends it, and Ahmad retires to Sārangpur, where he is treacherously attacked at night after terms of truce were agreed to on 12th *Muharram*, 826 (26th December).—B. G., 106.

1423 H. 826. Ahmad advances in April and defeats Hoshang Shāh.—B. G., 110.

1424 H. 827. Hoshang attacks the Rāja of Gwalior, on which Mubārāk Shāh proceeds against him, and plunders Hoshang's camp, who then sues for peace.—E. M. H., iv., 60. B. F., i., 617.

In an inscription at Deogarh Hoshang is called " Sri Alambhaka " of Mandapapura (Māndu).—J. A. B., lii., (i), 70.

1428 H. 832. Hoshang Shāh attacks Kherla, but is defeated by the Bāhmani king, Ahmad I.—B. F., iv., 183. I. A., xxviii., 152.

1429 H. 833. Mubārak Shāh captures Gwalior.—E. M. H., iv., 67.

A.D.

1433 H. 836. Mubarak Shāh II. sends Malik Kamāl-ul-Mulk against Gwalior.—E. M. H., iv., 75, 79. B. F., i., 527. T. P. K., 332.

1434 H. 837. Hoshang Shāh of Mālwa takes Kālpi. He dies at Māndu, where his tomb still stands. B. F., iv., 183, 189.

Ghazni Muhammad Khān succeeds Hoshang, till 1436.—B. M. C., *Muham. States*, 114, Int. liii. B. F., iv., 189. Nu. Chr., 1904, 356.

1435 H. 838. (8th July). Mahmūd Khilji I. murders Ghazni Khān and starts the Khilji dynasty of Mālwā. Masūd Khān, son of Ghazni Khān, flies to Gujarāt.—B. M. C., *Muham. States.* 114, Intr., lxvi. B. F., iv., 193.

1437 H. 841. Ahmad Shāh I. of Gujarāt beseiges Mahmūd of Mālwa in Māndu, and seizes Sārangpur, while Muhammad Umar Khān, a son of Hoshang Shāh, raises a revolt at Chanderi.—B. G., 123.

Ali-Rājpur and Jobat States founded.

1438 H. 842. Mahmūd Khilji marches on Sārangpur, where he kills Umar Khān. Cholera or plague in Ahmad's army forces him to retire.—B. G., 124.

Mahmūd then takes Chanderi and restores his power. —B. F., iv., 204.

1439 H. 843. Mahmūd of Mālwā then marches to Narwar, which had been attacked by Dungar Rai, Rāja of Gwalior, and relieves the fortress.—B. F., iv., 205.

Mahmūd this year builds a mosque near the Rāmpura Gate at Māndu.—B. F., iv., 205.

1440 H. 844. Mahmūd of Mālwā, invited by some Delhi nobles, advances to seize the capital, but is forced to retire by Bahlol Lodi.—E. M. H., iv., 85; v., 73. B. F., iv., 206.

V. Sam., 1497, 1510. Two inscriptions at Suhāniya (Gwalior), of Dungarendradeva (Dungar Singh) Tonwāra.—J. A. B., viii., 693; xxxi., 404, 422. C. A. S. R., ii., 400.

1441 H. 845. Mahmūd this year erects many buildings at Nālchha.—B. F., iv., 207.

Mahmūd defeats Nāzir Khān at Kālpi, and prevents his becoming independent. He then advances on Chitor against Rāna Kumbhakarna.—B. F., 207. I. A., i., 1.

Malik Mughīs, father of Māhmūd, dies at Mandasor. B. F., iv., 209.

1442 H. 846. Rāna Kumbhakarna attacks Mahmūd Khilji's camp outside Chitor, but the sorti failing he retires. The rains suspend operations.—B. F., iv., 207, 210.

1443 H. 847. *Zilhijja*, 25, (April 26). A fight takes place between the Rāna and Mahmūd, each claiming the victory. Rāna Kumbhakarna erects his "Jaya stambha" on Chitor fort, and Māhmūd a "seven storyed" tower at Māndu to commemorate the event.—T. P. K., 354. B. F., iv., 210. C. A. S. R., xxiii., 101. *Rājasthān*, i., 267.

A.D.

1445 H. 849. Mahmūd founds a hospital at Māndu.—B. F., iv., 214.

1444 H. 848. The Mālwā and Jaunpur rulers engage in war. —B. F., iv., 211.

1446 H. 850. Mahmūd Khilji again attacks the Rāna who however buys him off.—B. F., iv., 214.

1450 H. 854. Mahmūd assists the Rāja of Champanīr. –B. G., 130. I. A., i., 1.

1451 H. 855. Bahlol Lodi succeeds as Emperor.—T. P. K., 357.

Mahmūd Khilji invades Gujarāt, and Muhammad Karīm dies, but his son and successor Kutb-ud-dīn carries on the campaign and in March 1452 defeats Māhmūd.—B. G., 133–146. B. F., iv., 36. I. A., viii., 183.

1454 H. 858. Mahmūd founds (?) a town called Khiljipura after his clan near Mandasor. B. F., iv., 222.

1457 H. 861. Mahmūd is joined by Kutb-ud-dīn of Gujarāt in an attack on Rāna Kumbhakarna. Mahmūd is taken prisoner. According to the *Mirat-i-Sikandari*, however, Kutb-ud-dīn reduced Abu, and ultimately took Chitor.—B. G., 150. Nu. Chr., 1904, 16–19. T. P. K., 354. (*The two events of* 850 *and* 861 *seem here to be confused.*)

1462 H. 866. Mahmūd of Mālwā attacks Nizām Shāh Bāhmani, but retires on the approach of Mahmūd Baiqarah of Gujarāt, though he defeats the Bāhmani king first in a battle near Bīdar.—B. G., 175. B. F., ix., 468; iv., 224. I. A., xxviii., 152.

1463 H. 867. Mahmūd of Mālwā invades the Deccan up to Daulatābād.—B. G., 178.

1465 H. 870. Kherla, which had been seized by the Bāhmanis, was retored to Mahmūd by Muhammad II., Bāhmani. —I. A., xxviii., 152.

Envoys from the Khalīfa Muatajid Yūsuf, bring presents to Mahmūd. B. F., iv., 229.

1469 H. 874. Mahmūd of Mālwā dies on 1st June while invading Khīchiwāra. Under his rule Mālwā reached the zenith of its power. B. F., iv., 233.

Ghyās-ud-dīn his son succeeds, and gives himself up to luxury. His reign was only once disturbed by outside attack when Bahlol Lodi besieged Ranthambor (1482), and internally by the dissensions of his two sons, Nāsir-ud-dīn and Shujāat Khān.—B. F., iv,, 237. Nu. Chr., 1904, 376.

1488 H. 894. Rāja Mān Singh Tonwāra of Gwalior (or his son ?) submits to Bahlol Lodi.—E. M. H., v., 91, note.

1489 H. 894. Death of Bahlol Lodi and succession of Sikandar Lodi.—E. M. H., iv., 444; v., 91.

1492 H. 897. Sikandar Lodi sends a *Khilat* to Rāja Mān Singh of Gwalior.—E. M. H., v., 92.

A.D.

1494 H. 899. Sikandar attacks the Baghel chief of Rewah Raja Bhīra (Bhid.)—E. M. H., v., 94.

1499 H. 904. Sikandar Lodi again attacks the Rewah chief and advances as far as Bāndhogarh fort.—E. M. H., iv., 463.

1501 H. 905. 30th March. Nāsir-ud-dīn succeeds Ghyās-ud-dīn, whom some writers say he poisoned.—B. G., 221. E. M. H., vi., 349.

H. 906. 6th *Ramzān*. A refractory chief of Dholpur having taken refuge with the Gwalior rāja, Sikandar advances on the fort, but Mān Singh sends his son Bikramājīt as a hostage and terms are made.—E. M. H., iv., 466; v., 97.

Rudra Pratāp founds the Orchha State.

1502 H. 908. Nāsir-ud-dīn of Mālwā advances on Chitor, but is bought off.—B. F., iv., 243.

1505 H. 911. Sikandar's camp is attacked by the Gwalior Rājā. —E. M. H., v., 100.

1506 H. 912. Sikandar Lodi in reprisal ravages Gwalior territory and destroys numerous temples.—E. M. H., iv., 466.

1507 H. 913. Sikandar Lodi invests Narwar fort.—E. M. H., iv., 466; v., 102.

1509 H. 915. Muhammad Khān grandson of Nāsir-ud-dīn of Mālwā quarrels with his father and flies to Sikandar Lodi, who supports him at Chanderi.—E. M. H., v., 102, fort

1511 H. 916. 30th April. Death of Nāsir-ud-dīn and succession of Mahmūd Khilji II. to Mālwā. B. F., iv., 244.

1512 H. 917. Muzaffar II. of Gujarāt invades Mālwā. B. G., 250. Sikandar Lodi assists Buhjat Khān governor of Chanderi against Māhmūd of Mālwā. Buhjat transfers his allegiance to Delhi and makes over the fort to Sikandar.—E. M. H., iv., 467. B. F., i., 583.

1517 H. 923. *Zil-qādah* 4th (Nov. 18th) Muzaffar marches on Māndu and invests it. Mahmūd flies to Gujarāt.—B. G., 256.

Sikandar supports the claim of Husain, a converted Hindu, formerly named Rai Dungar, of Sheopur (Sūisūpur).—E. M. H., v., 104.

Sikandar dies and Ibrāhīm succeeds him.—E. M. H., iv., 471.

His brother Jalāl-ud-dīn disputes succes[illegible] is assisted by Azam Humāyun, but being defeated flies to Gwalior.—E. M. H., v., 9, 12.

1518 H. 924. Muzaffar takes Mandū.—B. G., 258.

Raja Mān of Gwalior dies, and Ibrāhīm attacks the fort but only captures the Bādalgarh outwork.—E. M. H. v., 13, and note, 486. B. F., i., 595.

A.D.

1519 H. 925. Mahmūd of Mālwā kills Bhīm Karan at Gāgron. The Rāna of Chitor attacks and captures Mahmūd but releases him.—B. G., 263. B. F., iv., 262.

1520 H. 927. December. Azam Humayum attacks Gwalior but is recalled.—E. M. H., v., 20.

1521 H. 927. Mandasor is beseiged by Muzaffar's general.—B. G., 273.

II.—THE MUGHAL PERIOD, 1526 TO 1707.

1526 H. 932. *Rajab 7th* (21st April) Bābar defeats Ibrahīm Lodi II. at Pānipat and founds the Mughal Empire in India.—B. Mem., 304. E. M. H., iv., 252. T.P.K., 376.

Bahādur Shāh succeeds to Gujarāt.—B. G., 280, 307.

Mālwā was at this time about the fourth principality in India.—E. M. H., iv., 260.

H. 933. Bābar in November obtains possession of Gwalior.—E. M. H., iv., 265. B. Mem., 345.

1527 H. 933. *Jamadi II.* 13. Bābar defeats Rāna Sanka of Chitor at Kanwaha, and so overawes the Rājputs.—E. M. H., iv., 268. B. Mem., 351–367.

H. 934. On 7th Jamadi II. (Friday, 27th September) he takes Chanderi. A vivid account is given in Bābar's Memoirs.—B. Mem., 376. E. M. H., iv., 277.

1528 Bābar visits Gwalior fort, writing a description of it.—B. Mem., 382. E. M. H., iv., 280.

1530 H. 937. 6th *Jamadi I.* (27th December). Bābar dies and Humāyun succeeds.

1531 Rāna Ratan Singh of Chitor is attacked by Mahmūd II. of Mālwā. His ally Bahādur Shāh of Gujarāt advances to his help, and defeating Mahmūd on 26th March annexes Mālwā. Mahmūd is put to death when trying to escape, and the dynasty of the Mālwā Sultāns ends.—B. F., iv., 267. B. G., 348 ff.

1532 Bahādur Shāh proceeds to Bhīlsa, where he destroys temples and erects mosques.—B. F., iv., 118. B. G., 358.

1533 Bahādur Shāh leaves Mālwā and attacks Chitor, and Humāyun advances on Gwalior.—E. M. H., v., 124.

Mālwā at this time became parcelled out into petty principalities held by Rājput and Muhammadan chiefs, Mallu Khān holding round Sārangpur, Sikandar Khān round Siwāns (in Bhopāl), and a Rājput Silhadi ruling over Bhīlsa and Raisen.

1534 H. 941. Humāyun attacks Bahādur Shāh at Mandasor. Bahādur Shāh flies to Māndu and is beseiged, retiring to Gujarāt, and Māndu falls to Humāyun.—E. M. H., v., 190; vi., 12.

1535 H. 942. Humāyun completes his conquest of Mālwā.—E. M. H., iv., 352; v., 191; vi., 13.

Bhopal Rai of Bījagarh seizes Māndu when Humāyun retires.—E. M. H., vi., 18.

A.D.

1539 Sher Shāh defeats Humāyun at Chaunsa.—E. M. H., iv., 374; v., 113.

1540 Final defeat of Humāyun by Sher Shāh on 16th May at Kanauj, the latter becoming Emperor of India.—E. M. H., iv., 375; v., 130, 143, 205. T. P. K., 392.

1542 Sher Shāh marches on Gwalior, which is surrendered to him.—E. M. H., iv., 391, 393.

Akbar is born at Umarkot on 15th October. E. M. H., v., 214.

1543 H. 950. Sher Shāh proceeds to settle Mālwā and ousts Mallu Khān, Puran Mal, and other petty rulers.—E. M. H., iv., 379, 391, 397, 404, 406; vi,, 118.

Sher Shāh makes Shujāat Khān (Shujāwal Khān) governor of Mālwā.—E. M. H., iv., 396.

1545 H. 952. Sher Shāh is killed at Kālanjar 22nd May. His younger son Jalāl Khān who was living at Rewah at the time, finally ousts his elder brother and succeeds as Islām Shāh.—E. M. H., iv, 408.

1546 H. 953. Adl Shāh, the elder brother, disputes the succession, but is defeated and flies into "Bahata" *i.e.* the Rewah country.—E. M. H., iv., 484.

1554 H. 962. Sikandar Shāh succeeds Islām Shāh.—E. M. H., v., 56.

1555 H. 963. Battle of Sirhind and return of Humāyun.—E. M. H., v, 58, 237.

Rājā Rām Chandra succeeds to Rewah State.

1556 H. 964. Humāyun dies on 20th January, and Akbar succeeds.—E. M. H., v., 240.

Suri power finally broken at Pānipat on 5th November.—E. M. H., v., 252.

1558 H. 966. Akbar sends Bahādur Khān to reduce Mālwā, where Bāz Bahādur, son of Shujāat Khān, is ruling.—E. M. H., v., 167, 168, 259, 493.

1559 Shaikh Muhammad Ghaus, the famous saint of Gwalior, visits Akbar at Agra —E. M. H., v., 260.

Gwalior fort surrended to Akbar.—E. M. H., v., 493.

1561 H. 968. Adham Khān Koka is sent to reduce Mālwā. He defeats Bāz Bahādur at Sārangpur where the famous singer Rup Mati commits suicide.—E. M. H., v., 270.

1562 Bāz Bahādur returns and seizes Māndu, defeating Pīr Muhammad Khān, Adham Khān's successor as governor. Later, however, he is completely defeated by Abdullah Khān Uzbek and submits.—E. M. H., v., 275 ff.

1564 H. 971. Akbar visits Narwar, Sārangpur, Māndu (*Zilhijja*—August). In *Muharram* 972 he returns to Agra *viâ* Nālchha and Sīpri.—E. M. H., v., 289, 291.

1567 H. 974. Chitor taken by Akbar.—E. M. H., v., 169, 325.

Asaf Khān takes Rāmpura (Indore)—*ibid* 171, 326.

Sheopur ("Supar") was also taken—*ibid*, 325.

A.D.

1572 The Jhābua State is founded about this time by Kesho Dās Rāthor.

1577 H. 985. An expedition is sent to bring Rājā Madhukar Sāh of Orchha to order.—E. M. H., vi., 57.

1579 H. 987. Akbar keeps his birthday feast at Depālpur (Indore).

1583 H. 991. Rājgarh State founded.

1584 Rājā Rām Chandra of Rewah visits Akbar.—E. M. H., v., 447, 538.

1591 H. 1000. Prince Murād becomes governor of Mālwā. He attacks Madhukar Sāh Rājā of Orchha, who flies into the jungles where he dies. Madhukar's son, Rām Chandra, is pardoned and succeeds.—E. M. H., v., 460.

1595 Famine in Mālwā.

1599 H. 1008. Akbar tours in Mālwā, visiting Gwalior (*Rabi II.*, 17th), 27th Sept.

1600 Akbar visits Sironj, Kaliādeh, Dhār (*14th Shabān*, 20th Feb. 1600), and Māndu (*21 Shabān*, 27th Feb. 1600).—E. M. H., vi., 134–146.

1602 H. 1010. *Rabi 17th* (Aug. 12th). Abul Fazl, author of the *Akbar-nāma*, is murdered near Antri in Gwalior by Bīr Singh Deo Bundela, afterwards Rājā of Orchha, at the instigation of Jahāngīr.—E. M. H., vi., 106, 108, 113, 154, 160, 288. Price. *Memoirs of Jahangueir* (1829), 32.

Akbar sends a force against Bīr Singh Deo. Orchha is taken, but he escapes. E. M. H., vi., 108, 113, 114.

1605 H. 1014. *20th Jamadi I.* (5th Oct.). Akbar dies, and Jahāngīr succeeds. Jahāngīr raises Bīr Singh Deo Bundela to the Orchha *gaddi*. *Orchha State Gazetteer.*

1612 First mention of Marāthās.—E. M. H., vi., 333.

1615 Sir Thomas Roe comes on an embassy to Jahāngir from James I. of England.—*See Sir Thomas Roe's Diary* (2 Vols.) in Hakluyt Society's series.

1616 Jahāngīr visits Māndu, and Sir T. Roe with him.—Roe's *Diary*. Price's *Mem. of Jahangueir*, 108. E. M. H., vi., 348.

1617 H. 1027. Jahāngīr strikes a silver *tanka* with legend. "After the conquest of the Deccan he came from Māndu to Gujarāt." Previous *tankas* were of copper.—E. M. H., vi., 355.

1619 H. 1029. Aurungzeb born.—E. M. H., vii., 213.

1621 H. 1031. Jahāngīr stays at Māndu.—E. M. H., vi., 377.

1623 H. 1033. Shāh Jahān rebels and seizes Māndu.—E. M. H., vi., 387.

1624 H. 1034. Shāh Jahān repents and submits.—E. M. H., vi., 396, 419.

1626 H. 1036. Jahāngir imprisoned by Mahābat Khān.
Datia State is founded by Bhagwān Singh Bundela.

A.D.

1627 H. 1037. *28 Safar* (Oct. 18). Jahāngīr dies and Shāh Jahān succeeds.—E. M. H., vi., 435; vii., 5.

1628 H. 1038. Rebellion of Khān Jahān Lodi. His escape through Bundelkhand is connived at by Jhujhār Singh, Rājā of Orchha.—E. M. H., vii., 7, 19.
In this year Shivaji the Marāthā is born.

1630 H. 1040. Khān Jahān Lodi trying to return through Central India is attacked by Jhujhār Singh and his son and defeated.—E. M. H., vii., 20.
Famine in part of Mālwā.

1632 V. Sam. 1688. Record of Mitragena from Rohtās fort. He was a scion of the Tonwāra family of Gwalior.—J. A. B., viii., 695.

1634. H. 1044. Jhujhār Singh of Orchha rebels, but is pursued by the Mughals, and flies to the jungles where he is killed by the Gonds.—E. M. H., vii., 47. J. A. B., vi., 262.
Orchha becomes *khālsa* territory till 1641.

1635 H. 1045. Shāh Jahān goes to Māndu in the rains.—E. M. H., vii., 57.

1636 H. 1046. The Bundelas attempt to set up Pirthi Rāj, son of Jhujhār Singh, as Rājā of Orchha.—E. M. H., vii., 61.

1640 H. 1050. Pirthi Rāj Bundela is captured and confined at Gwalior.—E. M. H., vii., 68.

1641 H. 1051. Shāh Jahān puts in Pahār Singh, a son of Bīr Singh Deo, as Rāja of Orchha.

1647 V. Sam, 1590. The Ratlām state is founded by Ratan Singh Rathor.

1658 H. 1068. Disturbances arise owing to quarrels of Shāh Jahān's sons. Battle of Fatehābād (or Dharmatpur) near Ujjain on *Rajab 22* (20th April), Ratan Singh, Raja of Ratlām is killed.—*Rājasthan*, ii., 47. E. M. H., vii., 219.

1659 Aurungzeb succeeds.

1666 H. 1070. *Rajab* (22nd Jan). Shāh Jahān dies.—E. M. H., vii., 275.

1671 H. 1082. Chhatarsāl of Panna commences to acquire territory and founds the Panna State.

1674 Shivaji Marāthā assumes royalty.

1675 Chhatarsāl Bundela settles at Panna and forms nucleus for the present State.

1680 Death of Shivaji.

1681 The Narsinghgarh State is founded.

1690 The Marāthās cross the Narbada for the first time.

1695 The Sītāmau State founded.

1698 H. 1110. Prince Muhammad Azam becomes governor of Mālwā.—E. M. H., vii., 369.

A.D.

1702 H. 1114. Marāthās ravage as far as Sironj, Ujjain, and Mandasor.—E. M. H., vii., 373, 375.

1705 The Marāthās cross the Narbada in great force and ravage Mālwā.—G. D., i., 340.

C.—The Marāthā Period, 1707 to 1818.

1707 H. 1119. 28 *Zilkaada* (4th March), Aurungzeb dies.
Battle of Jajau, where Prince Azam Shāh is killed and Bahādur Shāh succeeds.—E. M. H., vii., 395.

1709 Dost Muhammad founds Bhopāl State. (It is difficult to assign exact date, but *see* E. M. H., viii., 59.)

1714 Bālaji Wiswanāth becomes first Peshwa.—G. D., i., 371.

1717 Udaji Ponwār, afterwards founder of Dhār, is sent on an expedition to the Deccan.—G. D., i., 379.
The Marāthās get a firm footing in Mālwā.

1719 Muhammad Shāh succeeds at Delhi. Nizām-ul-mulk made governor of Mālwā.—G. D., i., 381.

1720 Bāji Rao I. becomes Peshwa.

1723. The Nizām retires from the governorship of Mālwā, and Holkar, Sindhia and the Ponwār firmly establish the Marāthā ascendancy in this province.

1725. Bāji Rao grants formal powers to Sindhia and Holkar to collect *chauth* in Mālwā.—G. D., i.. 419.

1728. Dost Muhammad founds Bhopāl city.
Dewās State (S. B. and J. B.) founded.
Malhār Rao Holkar is granted twelve districts in Mālwā and founds the Indore State. Sindhia acquires lands at the same time round Ujjain and founds Gwalior State.

1729 Dhār State founded by Udaji, Ponwār.
Muhammad Khān Bangash invades Bundelkhand, and Chhatarsāl of Panna calls in the Peshwa to aid him, thus establishing Marāthā ascendancy in Eastern Central India.—E. M. H., viii., 46.

1730 Sailāna State founded.

1731 Division of Bundelkhand by Chhatarsāl, forming numerous small States.

1733 Founding of Samthar State. The Marāthās were by this time well established in Mālwā.—G. D., i., 439–499.

1736 Bāji Rao applies for formal grant of power to collect *chauth* in Mālwā.—G. D., i., 450.

1738 Fight between the Nizām and Peshwa near Bhopāl. By resultant convention of Sarai Durai (? Barai) the Nizām makes over Mālwā to Bāji Rao.—G. D., i., 459.

1740 Bāji Rao I. Peshwa dies, and Baji Rao II. (Bālaji) succeeds.—G. D., i., 477.

A.D.

1743 Bāji Rao II. becomes Deputy Governor of Mālwā.—G. D., i., 499.

1745 Rānoji Sindhia dies at Shujālpur. Jāyapa Sindhia succeeds to Gwalior. Sindhia, Holkar, and the Ponwār become paramount in Mālwā.

1748 Ahmad Shāh succeeds Muhammad Shāh. Holkar and Sindhia take part in the Rohilla war.—G. D., i., 536.

1754 Ghāzi-ud-dīn blinds Ahmad Shāh and puts Alamgīr II. on the throne.

1756 Ahmad Shāh Abdāli sacks Delhi.

1757 Battle of Plassey, 23rd June.

1759 Jāyapa Sindhia assassinated at Nāgor.—G. D., i., 601. *Rajasthan*, i., 712; ii., 120.

1761 Battle of Pānipat, on 13th January, and defeat of Marāthās by Ahmad Shāh Abdāli.—G. D., i., 619. E. M. H., viii., 280. *Asiatic Researches*, iii., 91.

Mahādji Sindhia succeeds to Gwalior.

Bāji Rao II. (Bālaji) dies and is succeeded as Peshwa by Mādho Rao.—G. D., i., 621.

1763 Shāh Alam overruns Bundelkhand.—E. M. H., viii., 214.

1764 Founding of Charkhāri and Ajaigarh States.

Battle of Buxār, 23rd October.

1766 Death of Malhār Rao Holkar at Alampur. Mali Rao succeeds but dies soon after, and Ahalyā Bai rules (1767–1795).

1769 Bijāwar State founded.

1770 From 1770–1800 comparative peace reigned in Central India under Ahalya Bai Holkar (1767–95), and Tukoji Holkar, 1795–97.

Maihar State founded.

1771 Mādho Rao Peshwa dies and is succeeded by Narayan Rao.

1772 Murder of Narayan Rao, Raghunāth Rao (Raghoba) succeeding.—G. D., i., 698.

1773 The "Regulating Act" is passed, and Warren Hastings becomes the first Governor-General.

1774 Mādho Rao II. Peshwa succeeds Raghunāth Rao.—G. D., i., 714.

1778 Colonel Leslie commences march from Bengal to Bombay. He dies in October, and Colonel Goddard completes march. Is loyally assisted by the Bhopāl Darbār.—G. D., ii., 73–76, 98.

1780 Major Popham takes Lahār fort (February) and Gwalior fort (3rd August).—G. D., ii., 129–131.

1781 Major Camac defeats Sindhia at Sīpri (February). G. D., ii., 152. Sindhia makes overtures. G. D., ii., 159.

A.D.

1782 Treaty of Salbai with Sindhia (17th May). David Anderson appointed first Resident with Sindhia.—G. D., ii., 161.

1783 Orchha town abandoned as State capital in favour of Tīkamgarh.

1784 Sindhia receives title of Deputy *Vakīl-ul-mutlaq.*—G. D., ii., 180.

De Boigne enters Sindhia's service.

1785 Sindhia seizes Agra, and harrasses Khīchwāra. Great famine in Gwalior described by Mr. Malet.—G. D., ii., 183. *Malet's Diary*, given in *Selections from Bombay Records, Marātha Series.* Vol. I.

Chhatarpur State founded.

Warren Hastings retires and Sir John Macpherson officiates as Governor-General.

1786 Lord Cornwallis Governor-General (first time).

1788 Ghulām Kādir blinds Alam Shāh. Sindhia intervenes and is all powerful at Delhi.

1790 De Boigne wins battle of Pātan for Sindhia (20th June).

1792 De Boigne wins Merta (10th September). Sindhia carries out investiture of Peshwa as *Vakīl-ulmutlaq.*—G. D., ii., 254.

Tukoji Rao Holkar enlists services of Chevalier Dudrenec.—G. D., ii., 250.

Ali Bahādur and Himmat Bahādur conquer Bundelkhand.—G. D., ii., 251.

1793 Sir John Shore becomes Governor-General.

Battle of Lakheri in which De Boigne defeats Holkar. G. D., ii., 258.

1794 Death of Mahādji Sindhia and succession of Daulat Rao.—G. D., ii., 261.

1795 Death of Ahalya Bai Holkar and succession of Tukoji Rao I.

Sarji Rao Ghātke enters Sindhia's service.

Mādho Rao Peshwa commits suicide, and Bāji Rao III succeeds.—G. D., ii., 296, 312.

1796 De Boigne leaves Sindhia's service, and Perron gets command.

1797 Tukoji Rao Holkar I. dies, and dissensions arise in which Daulat Rao Sindhia joins. Jaswant Rao Holkar finally comes to the front.—G. D., ii., 356.

1798 The "Gardi-ki-wakt" commences in Central India, anarchy and confusion reigning everywhere till 1818. Pindāris become more and more numerous, their bands sweeping Central India, devastating the country and murdering the inhabitants.

Lord Wellesley becomes Governor-General.

1800 Nāna Farnavīs dies.

1801 Holkar attacks Ujjain.—G. D., ii., 358.

Sindhia retaliates on Indore (14th October).—G. D., ii., 361.

A.D.

1802 Holkar takes Poona. Peshwa signs the treaty of Bassein (31st December).

1803 Campaign against Sindhia in which his power is broken at Ahmadnagar (12th August), Aligarh (4th September), Delhi (11th September), Assaye (23rd September), Agra (10th October), Asīrgarh (21st October), Laswari (1st November), Argaon (28th November), and Gawilgarh (15th December). Treaty of Sarji-Anjangaon signed by Sindhia on 30th December. Bundelkhand is pacified.

Famine in Bundelkhand.

1804 Colonel Monson is defeated at the Mukandwāra Pass by Holkar.

Holkar defeated at Dig.

Treaty made with Datia State.

1805 Lord Cornwallis, Governor-General (second time).

Holkar makes terms and signs treaty of Rājpurghāt (24th December).

Gwalior and Gohad are restored to Sindhia.

Lord Cornwallis dies and Sir G. Barlow officiates. He leaves the Rājput States at the mercy of Holkar and Sindhia, and anarchy follows.

1806 Sanad granted to Chhatarpur State.

1807 Anarchy in Bundelkhand; Kālanjar fort taken.

Lord Minto arrives as Governor-General.

1809 Wazīr Muhammad becomes Nawāb of Bhopal.

Ajaigarh fort taken by Colonel Martindell.

1810 Daulat Rao Sindhia founds Lashkar city.

1811 Jaswant Rao Holkar dies insane, and Malhār Rao II. succeeds. Indore in a state of anarchy. Pindāri excesses increase in Central India.

Sanad granted to the Panna, Charkhāri, and Bijāwar States.

1812 Treaties made with Orchha and Rewah States, and *sanad* granted to Ajaigarh.

1813 Lord Hastings Governor-General.

1816 Nazar Muhammad succeeds as Nawāb of Bhopāl. All chiefs called on to assist in suppressing the Pindāris.

1817 Pindāri war.—T. Prinsep. *Administration of the Marquess Hastings* (*vide* Index).

Battle of Mehidpur (21st December). Treaty with Samthar State made.

D.—The Modern Period, 1818 to present day.

1818 Treaty of Mandasor with Holkar (20th January). Formation of the Jaora State under this treaty, with Ghafūr Khān as first Nawāb.

The pacification of Central India was commenced at this time and most agreements with the Native States date from this period.

The Peshwa surrenders to Sir J. Malcolm at Mhow.

A.D.
1819 Sikandar Begam succeeds at Bhopāl.

1826 First Opium Agreement with Indore, Dewās, Rātlam, &c.

1827 Death of Daulat Rao Sindhia and succession of Jānkoji.

1828 Lord W. Bentinck Governor-General.

1829 Second (and existing) Opium Agreement, with Native States.

Act passed abolishing Sati.

Famine in Bundelkhand.

1833 Severe famine in Bundelkhand.

1834 Agra-Bombay high road commenced.

1835 Suppression of Thagi in Central India by Colonel Sleeman.

1836 Lord Auckland Governor-General.

1839 Mr. L. Wilkinson opens the first school in Central India at Sehore.

1842 Lord Ellenborough Governor-General.

1843 Death of Jānkoji Rao Sindhia and succession of Jāyaji. Disturbances at Gwalior and British intervention ending in battles of Mahārājpur and Panniār (29th December). *See* Thornton's *History of India*, vi, 466 ff.

1844 Treaty of Gwalior (13th January) and raising of Gwalior Contingent.

Lord Hardinge Governor-General.

Tukoji Rao Holkar II. succeeds at Indore.

1848 Lord Dalhousie Governor-General.

The first hospital opened in Central India, at Indore.

1854 Annexation of Jhānsi State. Formation of the Central India Agency under Sir R. Hamilton, as first Agent.

1856 Lord Canning Governor-General.

1857 The Mutiny. Outbreaks at Gwalior and Morār (14th June), Sipri (18th June), Nowgong (24th June), Indore and Mhow (1st July), Bhopāwar (2nd July), Nīmach (3rd July), Agar (4th July), Nāgod (3rd September), and Mehidpur (8th November).

Mhow column march and take Dhār (29th October); fights at Mandasor (21st November), and Gurāria (24th November), and relief of Nīmach.

1858 Central India field force operates under Sir Hugh Rose (Lord Strathnairn).

Battle of Gwalior (18th June), and death of Lakshini Bai, Rānī of Jhānsi; Chanderi taken on St. Patrick's day.

1859 Capture and execution of Tantia Topi.

1862 Adoption Sanads securing succession, granted to all chiefs.

1872 Chiefs' College founded at Nowgong (was amalgamated with Daly College, Indore, in 1898).

1876 Classes for chiefs' sons started at Indore Residency School.

1877 Great Darbār at Delhi.

A.D.	
1878	Thagi and Dacoity Department reorganised under a General Superintendent. Salt agreement with Gwalior.
1881	Census (1st) taken. Salt agreements made between 1881 and 1883 with most States.
1886	Morār and Gwalior fort restored to Sindhia, in exchange for Jhānsi. Daly College for sons of chiefs opened.
1887	Chiefs undertake to raise Imperial Service Troops.
1891	Census (2nd) taken.
1897	Severe famine in Bundelkhand. Local Corps placed under Commander-in-Chief.
1899	Severe famine in all parts of Agency. Central India Agency Police formed.
1901	Census (3rd) taken.
1902	Coronation Darbār at Delhi.
1903	Local Corps delocalised.
1904	Abolition of Thagi and Dacoity Department, its work being done by the local administrations.
1905	Prince and Princess of Wales visit Indore.

NOTE ON ERAS USED IN CENTRAL INDIA.

Several eras are met with in inscriptions, copper-plates, &c., and some are still used by States in determining the official year. There are, among Hindus, the *Vikrama Samvat*, *Gupta* era, *Saka* and *Chedi*, and the *Hijra* and other Muhammadan forms of computing the year among Muslims.

A.—HINDU ERAS.

(i.) The *Vikrama Samvat** is the commonest mode of reckoning the year in Central India. It is a luni-solar or *Chandra-māna* year of twelve months with intercalary or *ādhika* (vulgo *lound*) months added as may be necessary. Both the common methods of reckoning are met with, viz. :—

(*a*) That followed generally in Northern India by which the year commences on the new moon immediately preceding the sun's entry into *Mesha* or Aries. The months are reckoned from full-moon to full-moon, whence it is known as the

* The origin of this era is disputed, but it is interesting to note that in the earliest instances of its employment it is termed "the era of the lords of Mālava," thus identifying it with the tract of this name.

purnimānta system. The epoch in this case dates from 14th March B.C. 57 or *Chaitra Sudi* 1st of the *Kali Yug* year 3044. The year's commencement now falls in March or April.

(*b*) That followed in Gujarāt and generally south of the Narbada, by which the year commences on the new moon in *Kārtik* (October—November). The months running from new-moon to new-moon, known as the *amānta* system. The epoch commences with 22nd September B.C. 57, corresponding to *Kartik Sudi* 1st of the *Kali Yug* year 3044.

Roughly speaking the Vikrama Samvat year *minus* 57 gives the year A.D.

Equation :—1966 − 57 = 1909.

(ii.) The *Gupta* or *Vallabhi* era is no longer used but is met with in records. It is a dynastic era of which the initial year corresponds to 320 A.D.

Equation :—Gupta year + 319 = year A.D.

(iii.) The *Saka* year is, nowadays, practically met with only in inscriptions, &c., in Central India. It is probably a sidereal year and commences with the vernal equinox. The epoch dates from the vernal equinox or *Chaitra Sud's* 1st of the *Kali Yug* year 3179, corresponding to March 14th, 78 A.D.

Equation :—Saka year + 78 = year A.D.

(iv.) The *Chedi* or *Kalachuri* era is used in old records only. It dates from 249 A.D.

Equation :—Chedi year + 249 = year A.D.

B.—MUSLIM ERAS.

(i.) The *Hijra* (A.H.). This is a simple lunar year and dates from Friday, July 15th, 622 A.D., the day of Muhammad's flight to Medina. The following equation will serve most purposes :—

(A.H. × 0·97) + 621·54 = year A.D.

When the decimal exceeds 0·5 add one year.

Equation :—A.H. 1327 × 0·97 = 1287·19
Add 621·54
1908·73

A.H. 1327 = 1909.

The next ten years will commence—

1327 on 1909, Jan. 23rd.	1332 on 1913, Nov. 30th.
1328 on 1910, Jan. 13th.	1333 on 1914, Nov. 19th.
1329 on 1911, Jan. 2nd.	1334 on 1915, Nov. 9th.
1330 on 1911, Dec. 22nd.	1335 on 1916, Oct. 28th.
1331 on 1912, Dec. 11th	1336 on 1917, Oct. 17th.

The difference is about 10 or 11 days yearly.

(ii.) The *Fasli* year is often used in State documents, that of Northern India being common [but *see* (iii.)] This era dates from 1556, and is a luni-solar year.

Equation :—Fasli year + 592 = year A.D.

(iii.) The *Mālwa San* or *Deccan Fasli* year is also common and is locally known by the first name. It appears to have come into Central India from the south, possibly with the Marāthas.

Equation :—Deccan Fasli + 590 = year A.D.

(iv.) The *Arabi San* or *Shahur* is almost invariably used in all early documents in Marātha States. It was introduced in Hijri 745 or 1342 A.D.

Equation :—Arabi San + 599 = year A.D.

(v.) *Muslim solar year.**—This mode of reckoning is now used by the Bhopāl State. It dates from 570 A.D., the year of Muhammad's birth, and is a luni-solar year, with twelve months called after the Zodiacal signs.

Equation :—M.S.Y. + 570 = year A.D.

For further information *see* Prinsep's "Useful Tables"; Warren, "Sankalita"; Cunningham, "Book of Indian Eras."

DYNASTIC LISTS.

M. R. = MAHARAJ-ĀDHIRĀJĀ.

THE PARAMĀRAS OF MĀLWĀ. 800—1300 A.D.

i.	Upendra-rājā	800—25
ii.	Vairasinha I.	825—50
iii.	Siyaka I.	850—75
iv.	Vākpati I.	875—914
v.	Vairasinha II.	914—41
vi.	Siyaka II. (Harsha)	941—973
vii.	M. R. Vākpati-rājā (Munja) II.	973—995
viii.	Sindhu-rājā	995—1010
ix.	M. R. Bhojadeva I.	1010—55
x.	Jayasinha I.	1055—59
xi.	Udayāditya	1059—81
xii.	Lakshmadeva	1081—1104
xiii.	M. R. Naravarman	1104—34

* I have been unable to trace the origin of this era.

xiv.	Yashovarman - -	- 1134—42
	Interregnum - - -	- 1142—55
xv.	Jāyavarman I. -	- 1142—60
	Period of Dual Rule -	- 1144—1216

A. Branch.		*B. Branch.*
(Jayavarman).	15	Ajayavarman.
xvi. Lakshmivarman.	16	Vindhyavarman.
xvii. Harischandra.	17	Subhatavarman.
xviii. Udayavarman.	18	Arjunavarman.

xix.	Devapāladeva (son of xviii.) -	- 1216—40
xx.	Jāyatugideva - -	- 1240—56
xxi.	Jāyavarman II. - -	- 1256—62
xxii.	Jāyasinhadeva II. - -	- 1261—80
xxiii.	Bhojadeva II. - - -	- 1280—1310
xxiv.	Jāyasinha III. - -	- 1310

THE CHANDELLAS OF JAJHOTI (BUNDELKHAND) 800—1288 A.D.

i.	Nannuka. }	
ii.	Vākpati. }	
iii.	Jāyasakti. } circ - -	- 800—900
iv.	Vijāyasakti. }	
v.	Rāhila }	
vi.	M. R. Harsha - - -	- 900—925
vii.	M. R. Yashovarman - -	- 925—954
viii.	M. R. Dhanga -	- 954—1002
ix.	Ganda - - -	- 1002—25
x.	M. R. Vidyādhara - -	- 1025—37
xi.	M. R. Vijayapāla - -	- 1037—50
xii.	M. R. Devavarman - -	- 1050—98
xiii.	M. R. Kīrtivarman -	- 1098—1100
xiv.	Sallakshavarman - -	- 1100—17
xv.	Jāyavarman - -	- 1117—23
xvi.	M. R. Prithvivarman - -	1123—29
xvii.	M. R. Madanavarman -	- 1129—62
xviii.	Pratāpavarman - -	- (?)
xix.	Yasovarman - -	- (?)
xx.	M. R. Parmārdideva (Parmāl) -	- 1167—1202
xxi.	M. R. Trailokyavarman -	- 1202—41
xxii.	M. R. Vīravarman -	- 1241—86
xxiii.	Bhojavarman - - -	- 1286—90

MUHAMMADAN RULERS.

Pathan Kings.

Mahmūd of Ghazni - - - 998—1030 A.D.

Muiz-ud-dīn Muhammad Ghori - - 1174—1206

Kutb-ud-dīn Aibak - - - - 1206
Altamsh - - - - - 1210
Firoz I. (Rukn-ud-dīn) - - - 1236
Raziyat-ud-dīn - - - - - 1236
Bahram (Muiz-ud-dīn) - - - 1240
Masūd (Ala-ud-dīn) - - - - 1242
Nāsir-ud-dīn Mahmud - - - 1246
Ghiās-ud-dīn Balban - - - - 1266
Kaikobad (Muiz-ud-dīn) - - - 1286

Khiljis.

Jalāl-ud-dīn Firoz II. - - - - 1290
Alā-ud-dīn - - - - - 1296
Shihāb-ud-dīn - - - - - 1316
Kutb-ud-dīn Mubārak Shāh - - - 1316
Nāsir-ud-dīn Khusrū Shāh - - - - 1320

Tughlak Dynasty.

Ghyas-ud-dīn Tughlak - - - - 1320
Muhammad-ibn-Tughlak - - - - 1325
Tughlak Shāh - - - - 1351
Firoz Shāh III. - - - - - 1351
Abu-Bakr - - - - - 1388
Muhammad Shāh - - - - - 1389
Sikandar Shāh - - - - 1394
Mahmūd Shāh - - - - - 1394
Nasrat Shāh - - - - 1395
Mahmūd Shāh (restored) - - - - 1399
Daulat Khān Lodi - - - - 1412

Sayad Dynasty.

Khizr Khān - - - - - - - 1414
Mubārak Shāh - - - 1421
Muhammad Shāh - - - - - - 1434
Alim Shāh - - - - - 1451

Lodi Dynasty.

Bahlol Lodi	1451
Sikandar Lodi	1489
Ibrahīm Lodi	1517

(Bābar's invasion 1526.)

The Suri Dynasty.

Sher Shāh	1540
Islām Shāh	1545
Adil Shāh	1554
Ibrahīm Sūr	1554
Sikandar Shāh	1554

(Mughal conquest.)

The Mughal Dynasty,

Bābar	1526
Humāyun	1530
(*Suri dynasty*	1540—54)
Humāyun restored	1555
Akbar	1556
Jahāngir	1605
Shāh Jahān	1627
Aurungzeb Alamgir	1658
Bahādur Shāh	1707
Jahāndar Shāh	1712
Farokhsiyar	1713
Muhammad Shāh	1719
(Ahmad Shāh Durrāni invades India	1748)
Ahmad Shāh	1748
Alamgīr II.	1754
Shāh-Alam	1759
Akbar Shāh II.	1806
Bahādur Shāh II.	1837

THE SULTĀNS OF MĀLWĀ.

Ghoris.

Dilāwar Khān	1401
Hoshang Shāh	1405
Ghazni Khān	1435

Khiljis.

Mahmūd I.	1435
Ghyās-ud-dīn	1475
Nāsir-ud-dīn	1501
Mahmūd II.	1511
(Mālwā annexed by Bahādur Shāh of Gujarāt	1531)

AGENTS TO THE GOVERNOR-GENERAL IN CENTRAL INDIA.

Sir R. Hamilton	1854—59
Sir R. Shakespear	1859—61
Sir R. Meade	1861—69
Sir H. Daly	1869—81
Sir L. Griffin	1881—88
Mr. F. Henvey	1888—90
Mr. R. Crosthwaite	1891—94
Colonel D. Barr	1894—1900
Mr. C. S. Bayley	1900—05
Colonel H. Daly	1905

CHIEFS OF GWALIOR.

Rānoji Sindhia	d. 1745
Jāyapa	1745
Jānkoji I.	1759
Mahādji	1761
Daulat Rao	1794
Jānkoji Rao II.	1827
Jāyaji Rao	1843
Mādho Rao	1886

CHIEFS OF INDORE.

Malhār Rao Holkar	d. 1766
Male Rao	1766
Ahalyā Bai	1767
Tukoji Rao I.	1795
Kāshi Rao	1797
Jaswant Rao	1798
Malhār Rao II.	1811
Mārtand Rao	1833
Hari Rao	1834
Khande Rao	1843
Tukoji Rao II.	1844
Shivaji Rao	1886
Tukoji Rao III.	1903

The Peshwas.

1.	Bālaji Vishvanāth	1714
2.	Bāji Rao (I.) Ballāl	1720
3.	Balaji Bāji Rao (II.)	1740
4.	Mādhava Rao (I.) Ballal	1761
5.	Narayan Rao	1772
6.	Raghunāth Rao (Ragoba)	1772
7.	Mādhava Rao (II.) Narayan	1774
8.	Bāji Rao (III.) Raghunāth	1795—1817

N.B.—No. 6 was never invested by the Peshwa, but usurped the position.

Nos. 2, 3, and 8 are often called Bāji Rao only, and Nos. 4 and 7 Mādhava Rao. *See* "Selections from the Satara Rajas and Peshwas Diaries," by D. B. Parasnīs, Vol. I., 42.

CHRONOLOGICAL LIST OF RECORDS FOUND IN, OR DEALING WITH, CENTRAL INDIA.

All dates are in Vikrama Samvat unless otherwise indicated:—K. = Kalachuri; G. = Gupta; H. = Hijri; Ha. = Harsha S. = Saka; N.D. = Not dated (in this case an approximate date is given).

Dynasties:—Chand.=Chandella; Chāl.=Chālukyas; Chaul.=Chaulukyas of Anhilwāra; Gu.=Gupta; Kachh.=Kachchhapagnāta; Kal.=Kalachuris of Chedi; Kan.=Kanauj; Par.=Paramāras; Rāsh.=Rāshtrakūta; Val.=Vallabhi; Local=of local interest; Māl. S.=Mālwā Sultāns.

Year. A.D.	Samvat.	Inscriptions.	Reference.	Dynasties mentioned.
360	N.D.	Allāhābād pillar insc. of Samudragupta	C.I.I., iii, 1	Mālavas, Nāgas Abhīras, &c.
401	G. 82	Udayagiri cave insc.	C.I.I., iii, 21	Gupta.
401	N.D.	Udayagiri insc. of Chandragupta II.	C.I.I., iii, 35	Gupta.
412	G. 93	Sānchī convent insc.; time of Chandragupta II.	C.I.I., iii, 31	Gupta.
422	K. 174	Kārītalāī plates of Jayānātha	C.I.I., iii, 118	Uchchakalpa.
423	480	Gangrār insc. of Visvavarman of Mālwā	C.I.I., iii, 74	Local chief.
425	G. 106	Udayagiri Jaina insc.	C.I.I., iii, 258	Gupta.
425	K. 177	Khoh plates of Jayanātha	C.I.I., iii, 177; I.A., xix, 227	Uchchakalpa.
437	493	Mandasor insc. of Bandhuvarman	I.A., xviii, 227	Gupta.
441	K. 193	Khoh plates of Sarvanātha	C.I.I., iii, 126; I.A., xix, 227	Uchchakalpa.
445	K. 197	Khoh plate of Sarvanātha	C.I.I., iii, 133	Uchchakalpa.
450	G. 131	Sānchī insc.	C.I.I., iii, 261	Gupta.
462	K. 214	Khoh plates of Sarvanātha	C.I.I., iii, 136	Uchchakalpa.
473	529	Mandasor insc. of Bandhuvarman; 2nd part	I.A., xviii, 227	Gupta.
475	G. 156	Khoh plates of Hastin, Parivrājaka	C.I.I., iii, 95	Local chief.
482	G. 163	Khoh plates of Hastin, Parivrājaka	C.I.I., iii, 102	Local chief.
482	N.D.	Bhumara pillar insc. of Hastin and Sarvanātha	C.I.I., iii, 111	Local chief.
484	G. 165	Eran pillar insc. of Budhagupta	C.I.I., iii, 89	Gupta.

511	G. 191	Majhgawān plates of Hastin Parivrājaka	C.I.I., iii, 107	Local chief.
511	—	Eran sati insc. of Bhānugupta	C.I.I., iii, 92	Gupta.
520	N.D.	Eran boar insc. of Toramāna Huna	C.I.I., iii, 159	Gupta, Huna.
525	N.D.	Gwalior insc. of Mihirakula Huna	C.I.I., iii, 162	Gupta, Huna.
528	G. 209	Khoh plates of Sankshobha Parivrājaka	C.I.I., iii, 114	Local chief.
533	N.D.	Mandasor pillar insc. of Yasodharman	C.I.I., iii, 146; I.A., 222, 245, 252.	Hunas.
533	589	Mandasor well insc. of Yasodharman	C.I.I., iii, 152; I.A., 222, 245, 252	Hunas.
639	G. 320	Ratlām plates of Dhruvasena II., Val.	E.I., viii, 188.	Valabhi.
640	G. 321	Ratlām plates of Dhruvasena II., Val.	E.I., viii, 188	Valabhi.
713	770	Chitor insc. of the Mansarovar lake	Rājasthān, i, 751	Par.
808	S. 730	Rādhanpur plates of Govindarāja	I.A., vi, 242	Par.
861	917	Pathārī pillar insc. of Parabala	W.Z.K.M., 1901, 519	Rāsh. Local.
862	932	Gwalior insc. of Bhojadeva, Kan.	E.I., i, 154	Kan. Gurjara.
863	933	Gwalior insc. of Bhojadeva, Kan.	E.I., i, 159	Kan. Gurjara.
900	N.D.	Khajrāho insc. of Chandella's	E.I., i, 122	Chand.
900	N.D.	Khajrāho insc. of Harsha Chand.	E.I., l. 122	Chand.
903	960	Terahi insc. of Gunarāja	I.A., xvii, 202	Local.
903	960	Siyadoni insc. Dates from 903 to 968	E.I., i, 173	Kanauj.
950	N.D.	Dudahi insc. of Devalabhi Chand.	I.A., xviii, 237	Chand.
955	1011	Khajrāho insc. of Dhanga, Chand.	E.I. i, 124	Chand.
955	1011	Khajrāho Jaina insc. of Dhanga	E.I. i, 136	Chand.
956	1013	Suhaniya insc. of Mahendrachandra	J.B.A., xxxi., 399	Local chief
973	K. 724	Chandrehi insc. of Prasāntasiva	I.A., xx., 85	Local.
973	N.D.	Ranod insc. of Avantivarmam	E.I., i, 354	Local.
974	1031	Dharampuri plates of Vākpati II., Par.	I.A., vi, 51	Par.
975	N.D.	Bilhari insc. of Yuvarāja II., Kal.	E.I., i, 254	Par. Kal. Chaul.
977	1034	Gwalior insc. of Vajradāman, Kachh.	J.B.A., xxxi., 393	Gwalior dyn.
979	1036	Ujjain plates of Vākpati II., Par.	I.A., xiv., 160	Par.
982	S. 904	Nilgund insc. of Taila II., Chāl.	E.I., iv, 206	Par. Chāl.
996	N.D.	Insc. of Taila II., Chāl.	I.A., xxi, 167	Par Chāl.
997	1053	Bījapur insc. of Dhavala of Hastikundi	J.B.A., lxii (i), 311	Par.
998	1054	Nanyaura plate of Dhanga, Chand.	I.A., xvi, 202	Chand.
1000	S. 922	Sangamer plates of the Yādava, Bhillama II.	E.I., ii, 217	Par.

Year. A.D.	Samvat.	Inscriptions.	Reference.	Dynasties mentioned.
1001	1058	Kharjrāho insc. of Kokalla, Grahapati	E.I., i, 148	Local. Chand.
1002	1059	Khajrāho insc. of Dhanga, Chand.	E.I., i, 140	Chand.
1009	S. 930	Kauthem plates of Vikramāditya V., Chāl.	I.A., xvi, 27	Par. Chāl.
1021	1078	Ujjain plates of Bhoja I, Par.	I.A., vi, 53	Par.
1022	S. 941	Belgamve insc. of Jayasinha Western, Chāl.	Mysore insc., No. 72, 148	Par.
1038	K. 789	Piāwan rock insc. of Gāngeya, Kal.	C.A.S.R., xxi, 113	Local. Kal.
1042	K. 793	Benares plates of Karna, Kal.	E.I., ii, 305	Kal. Par. Chand.
1042	N.D.	Karanbel insc. of Jayasinha, Kal.	I.A., xviii, 216	Par. Kal.
1050	1107	Nanyaura plate of Devavarman, Chand.	I.A., xvi, 205	Chand.
1055	1112	Mandhāta plates of Jayasinha I., Par.	E.I., iii, 48	Par.
1059	1116	Udayapura insc. of Udayāditya, Par.	J.A.B., ix, 549	Par.
1060	1117	Bhinmal insc. of Krishnarāja, Par.	Bom. Gaz. I. (i), 472, No. iv	Par.
1067	1123	Bhinmal fragment of Krishnarāja, Par.	Bom. Gaz. I. (i), 473, No. v.	Par.
1070	N.D.	Insc. of Rajendra Choladeva II.	South Ind. Insc., iii, No. 64, 133	Par.
1077	1134–5	Kahla plates of Sodhadeva, Kal.	E.I., vii, 85	Kal.
1080	N.D.	Prashasti at Udayapura, of Paramāras	E.I., i, 233	Par. General account.
1080	1136	Arthūna insc. of Chāmundarāja, Par.	I.A., xxii, 80	Par.
1080	1137	Udayapura insc. of Udayāditya, Par.	I.A., xx, 83	Par.
1088	1145	Dubkund insc. of Vikramasinha, Kachh.	E.I., ii, 237	Par. Chand. Kan.
1093	1150	Sāsbahū insc. of Mahīpāla, Kachh.	I.A., xv., 36	Local. Gwalior dyn.
1095	1152	Dubkund Jaina pillar insc.	C.A.S.R., xx, 102	Local.
1097	1154	Plate of Madanapāla of Kanauj	I.A., xviii, 11	Kan. Par.
1098	1154	Deogarh insc. of Kīrtivarman, Chand.	I.A., xviii, 238	Chand.
1098	N.D.	Mahoba insc. of Kīrtivarman, Chand.	E.I., i, 221	Chand. Par. Kal.
1104	1161	Nāgpur insc. of Naravarman, Par.	E.I., ii, 80	Par. Kal.
1104	1161	Gwalior insc. of Mahīpāla, Kachh.	I.A. xv, 202	Local.
1107	1164	Madhukargarh insc. of Naravarman, Par.	Tr. R.A.S., i, 226	Par.
1107	N.D.	Sarpabhandhi insc. at Dhār and Un	J.B.R.A.S., xxi, 350; *Dhār State Gazetteer.*	Par.
1115	N.D.	Srāvana Belgola insc. of Prabhachandra	Srav. Bel. Insc., 55, pp. 47	Par.
1117	1173	Khajrāho insc. of Jayavarman, Chand.	E.I., i, 147	Chand.

1118	S. 1039	Insc. of the Hoysala, Ereyanga	Mysore Insc., Nos. 146, 260	Par.
1120	1177	Narwar insc. of Virasinha, Kachh.	J.A.O.S., vi, 542	Local.
1129	1186	Kālanjar insc. of Madanavarman, Chand.	C.A.S.R., xxi, 34	Chand.
1129	N.D.	Mau insc. of Madanavarman, Chand.	E.I., i, 197	Chand.
1130	1187	Kālanjar pillar insc. of Madanavarman, Chand.	C.A.S.R., xxi, 34	Chand.
1131	1188	Kālanjar rock insc. of Madanavarman, Chand.	C.A.S.R., xxi, 35	Chand.
1133	1190	Ignoda insc. of Vijayapāla (? Par.)	I.A., vi, 55	Par.
1133	1190	Augāsi plate of Madanavaram, Chand.	I.A., xvi, 207	Chand.
1133	1191	Dhār grant of Yasovarmam, Par.	I.A., xix, 353	Par.
1135	1192	Ujjain plates of Yasovarman, Par.	I.A., xix, 349	Par.
1140	1196	Dohad insc. of Jayasinha, Chaul.	I.A., x, 159	Par.
1142	N.D.	Ujjain plate of Jayavarman I, Par.	I.A., xix, 350	Par.
1144	1200	Ujjain plate of Lakshmivarman, Par.	I.A., xix, 352	Par.
1149	1205	Khajrāho Jain temple insc. of Grahapati's	E.I., i, 153	Local.
1151	1208	Ajaigarh insc. of Madanavarman, Chand.	C.A.S.R., xxi, 49	Chand.
1152	1208	Vadnagar prashasti of Kumārapāla, Chaul.	E.I., i, 296	Pr. [illegible]
1152	1208	Jain image inscription of Grahapati's	J.R.A.S., 1898, 101	Local.
1153	1210	Ajmer insc. of Vigraharāja, Chauhān	I.A., xx, 210	Par.
1155	K. 907	Bhorghāt insc. of Alhanadevi, Kal.	E.I., ii, 10	Kal. Par.
1155	1211	Mahoba image insc. of Madanavarman, Chand	C.A.S.R., xxi, 73	Chand.
1158	1215	Khajrāho image insc. of Grahapati's	E.I., i, 153	Chand.
1158	K. 909	Lālpahār insc. of Narasinha, Kal.	I.A., xviii, 212	Kal.
1159	1216	Alhaghāt insc. of Alhanadevi, Kal.	I.A., xviii, 214	Kal. Par.
1159	S. 1081	Srāvaha Belgola insc. of the Hoysala Ereyanga	Srāv. Bel. Insc., No. 139, 106	Par.
1162	1219	Varidurga plates of Madanavarman, Chand.	E.I., iv, 158	Chand.
1163	1220	Udayapura insc. of Kumārapāla, Chaul.	I.A., xviii, 341	Chaul. Par.
1163	1220	Udayapura pillar insc.	I.A., xviii, 344	Chaul. Par.
1167	1223	Semra plates of Paramardideva, Chand.	E.I., iv, 157	Chand.
1168	1224	Mahoba image insc. of Paramardideva, Chand.	C.A.S.R.., xxi, 74	Chand.
1169	G. 850	Verāval insc. of Bhāva-Brihaspati	W.Z.K.M., iii, 7	Chaul. Par.
1171	1227	Insc. from gate at Ajaigarh	C.A.S.R., xxi, 49.	
1171	1228	Ichchhāwar plates of Paramardideva, Chand.	I.A., xxv, 206	Chand.
1173	1229	Udayapura insc. of Ajayapāla, Chaul.	I.A., xviii, 347	Chaul. Par.
1175	K. 926	Rewah plate of Kīrtivarman of Kakkaredi	I.A., xvii, 226	Kal. Local.

Year. A.D.	Samvat.	Inscriptions.	Reference.	Dynasties mentioned.
1178	1235	Piplianagar plates of Harischandra, Par.	J.B.A., vii, 736	Par.
1179	1236	Piplianagar plates of Harischandra, Par.	J.B.A., vii, 736	Par.
1182	1239	Madanpur insc. of Paramardideva, Chand.	C.A.S.R., x, 173	Chand.
1184	1240	Kālanjar rock insc. of Paramardideva, Chand.	I.A., xix, 37	Chand.
1187	1243	Ajaigarh gate insc.	C.A.S.R., xxi, 50.	
1195	1252	Bagrāri insc. of Paramardideva, Chand.	E.I., i, 208	Chand.
1195	1253	Rewah plate of Sallakshanavarman, of Kakkredi	I.A., xviii, 228	Kal. Chand.
1200	N.D.	Jhansi insc. of Sallakshanasinha	E.I., i, 215	Chand. Par.
1200	1256	Bhopāl plates of Udayavarman, Par.	I.A., xvi, 254	Par.
1201	1258	Kālanjar insc. of Paramardideva, Chand.	J.B.A., xvii (i), 313	Chand.
1209	1265	Abu insc. of Dhāravarsha of Chandrāvatī, Par.	I.A., xxi, 221	Par. Chaul.
1211	1267	Piplianagar plates of Arjunavarman, Par.	J.B.A., v, 378	Par.
1213	1269	Ajaigarh insc. of Trailokyavarman, Chand.	C.A.S.R., xxi, 50	Chand.
1213	1270	Bhopāl plates of Arjunavarman, Par.	J.A.O.S., vii, 32	Par.
1215	1272	Bhopāl plates of Arjunavarman, Par.	J.A.O.S., vii, 24	Par.
1218	1275	Harsauda insc. of Devapāla, Par.	I.A., xx, 311	Par.
1223	1280	Kadi plates of Jayantasinha of Gujarāt	I.A., vi, 196	Par.
1225	1282	Mandhāta plates of Devapāla, Par.	E.I., ix, 103	Par.
1229	1286	Udayapura insc. of Devapāla, Par.	I.A., xx, 83	Par.
1230	1287	Abu insc. of Somasinha, Par.	Kathvate-*Kirtikaumudi*, App.	Par.
1230	1287	Abu insc. of Vīradhavala, Vaghela	Kathvate-*Kirtikaumudi*, App.	Par.
1232	1289	Udayapura insc. of Devapāla, Par.	I.A., xx, 83	Par.
1239	1297	Rewah plates of Kumarapāla, of Kakkredi	I.A., xvii, 231	Chand.
1241	1298	Rewah plates of Harirāja, of Kakkredi	I.A., xvii, 235	Chand.
1256	1312	Rāhatgarh insc. of Jayavarman (Jayatugi), Par.	I.A., xx, 84	Par.
1256	1313	Mori (unpublished) insc. of Jayavarman II., Par.	- - -	Par.
1260	1317	Plates of Jayavarman II., Par.	E.I., ix, 117	Par.
1261	1317	Ajaigarh insc. of Vīrvarman, Chand.	E.I., i, 327	Chand. Kal.
1261	N.D.	Kālanjar insc. of Vīrvarman, Chand.	J.B.A., xvii, i, 317	Chand. Kal.
1262	1318	Jhansi insc. of Vīrvarman, Chand.	- - - -	Chand.
1266	S. 1188	Insc. of Ravivarman (alludes to Bhoja, Par.)	E.I., iv, 149	Par.

1268	1325	Ajaigarh insc. of Vīrvarman, Chand.	I.A., xxi, 51	Chand.
1269	1326	Pathāri insc. of Jayasinha II., Par.	- - - -	Par.
1273	S. 1193	Paithān plates of Ravivarman	I.A., xiv, 315	Par.
1281	1337	Ajaigarh insc. of Vīrvarman, Chand.	C.A.S.R., xxi, 52	Chand.
1281	1337	Dāhi plates of Vīrvarman, Chand.	C.A.S.R., xxi, 74	Chand.
1283	1340	Kālanjar insc.	I.A., xix, 31.	Chand. (?)
1286	1342	Gurha insc. of Vīrvarman, Chand.	Unpublished	Chand.
1287	1343	Cintra prashasti of Sārangdeva, Vaghela	E.I., i, 271	Par. Vāghela.
1289	1345	Ajaigarh insc. of Bhojavarman, Chand	J.B.A., vi, 882	Chand.
1289	N.D.	Ajaigarh rock insc. of Bhojavarman, Chand.	E.I., i, 333	Chand.
1292	1348	Sarwaya insc. of Ganapati, of Narwar	I.A., xxii, 82	Local.
1296	S. 1217	Orissa plates of Narasinha II.	J.B.A., lxvi, 235	Par. (?)
1298	1355	Narwar insc. of Ganapati, of Narwar	I.A., xxii, 81	Local.
1310	1366	Udayapura insc. of Jayasinha III., Par.	I.A., xx, 84	Par.
1310	1387	Abu insc. of Tejasinha, Chauhān	A.S.W.I., ii, App. xv, No. 58	Par.
1315	1372	Ajaigarh insc. on a gate	C.A.S.R., xxi, 54	Chand. (?)
1322	1380	Udayapura insc.	I.A., xix, 28	Par. (?)
1333	1390	Kevati kund pillar insc.	C.A.S.R., xxi, 143	Local.
1338	1394	Insc. from Udayapura	I.A., xix, 355	Par. (?)
1338	1394	Abu insc. Kanhadeva of Chandrāvatī	I.A., ii, 256	Par.
1340	1397	Kevati kund insc. of Hamīradeva	C.A.S.R., xxi, 143	Local.
1348	1404	Rāmpur (Rewah) insc. of Vīrarāja	C.A.S.R., ix, 34; Pl. ii, 3	Local.
1355	1412	Kāritalāi insc. of Vīravarma, of Uchahadanagar	C.A.S.R., ix	Local.
1405	H. 808	Māndu insc. of Dilāwar Khān Ghori on mosque	J.B.R.A.S., xx, 384	Māl. S.
1405	H. 808	Dhār insc. of Dilāwar Khān, Ghori	J.B.R.A.S., xx, 347	Māl. S.
1406	H. 809	Māndu (Tārapur gate) insc. of Dilāwar Khān	J.B.R.A.S., xx, 381	Māl. S.
1410	1461	Gwalior insc. of Virangadeva, Tonwāra	J.B.A., xxxi, 422	Local. Gwalior dyn.
1424	1481	Deogarh insc. of Sāhi Alambhaka (Hoshang Shāh)	J.B.A., lii, 70	Māl. S.
1432	H. 835	Mandu insc. of Malik Mughis	J.B.R.A.S., xx, 387	Māl. S.
1440	1496	Suhaniya insc. of Dungarenda, Tonwāra	J.B.A., xxxi, 422	Local. Gwalior dyn.
1440	1496	Sādadi insc. of Kumbhakarna	Bhāvnagar insc., 114.	Māl. S.
1447	1503	Udayapura insc.	I.A., xix, 168	Par. (?)
1453	H. 857	Dhār insc. of Mahmud Khilji I.	J.B.R.A.S., xx, 352	Māl. S.
1454	1510	Suhaniya insc. of Dungarendra, Tonwāra	J.B.A., xxxi, 423	Local.

Year. A.D.	Samvat.	Inscriptions.	Reference.	Dynasties mentioned.
1454	H. 858	Māndū insc. of Mahmūd Khilji I.	J.B.R.A.S., xx, 385	Māl. S.
1457	H. 1000	Dhār, Lāt insc. of Akbar	J.B.R.A.S., xx, 348	Local.
1509	H. 914	Māndu insc. of Nāsir-ud-dīn, Khilji	J.B.R.A.S., xx, 388	Mal. S.
1517	H. 381	Māndu (Bhagwānia gate) insc. of Mirza Muhhammad	J.B.R.A.S., xx, 380	Māl. S.
1574	H. 982	Māndu insc. of Budagh Khān	J.B.R.A.S., xx, 390	Māl. S.
1591	H. 1000	Māndu insc. of Akbar	J.B.R.A.S., xx, 390	Local.
1591	H. 1000	Dhār insc. of Akbar	J.B.R.A.S., xx, 348	Local.
1600	H. 1609	Māndu insc. of Akbar	J.B.R.A.S., xx, 390	Local.
1632	1688	Rohtāsgarh insc. of Mitragena Tonwāra	J.B.A., viii, 695	Local, Gwalior dyn.
1668	H. 1079	Māndu (Alamgīr gate) insc.	J.B.R.A.S., xx, 379	Local.

GENERAL INDEX.

[Where a double reference occurs, that to the Chronology is shown in *italic type*. In all references to the Bibliography the number of the book or paper is given as well as that of the page.]

INDEX OF AUTHORS.